# MICROSOFT SURFACE PRO 10 5G FOR BEGINNERS 2024

*Step by step guide for Beginners to*

*Master the Microsoft Surface Pro 10*

## William G. Potter

# Table of Contents

# How To Add Custom Resolutions To The System Resolution List?

# INTRODUCTION

Welcome to the world of the Microsoft Surface Pro 10! In this digital era, where technology has become an integral part of our daily lives, the Surface Pro 10 stands as a versatile and innovative device that combines the power of a laptop with the convenience of a tablet. Whether you are a student, a professional, or a creative enthusiast, this user-friendly guide aims to provide you with a solid foundation of knowledge to make the most of your Surface Pro 10.

Surface pro 10 is designed to bridge the gap between functionality and portability, the Surface Pro 10 offers a remarkable array of features and capabilities. From its sleek design to its advanced hardware, this device empowers users to work, create, and connect in ways never imagined before. However, navigating a new device can be overwhelming, especially for beginners. That's where this guide comes in.

This book serves as your comprehensive companion, assisting you in unlocking the full potential of your Surface Pro 10. We will start with the basics, introducing you to the device's physical components, such as the display, keyboard, and pen. You will learn how to set up your Surface Pro 10, connect to Wi-Fi, and personalize your settings to suit your preferences.

As we delve deeper, we will explore the operating system, Windows 11, which powers the Surface Pro 10. You will familiarize yourself with the user interface, discover essential gestures and shortcuts, and understand how to navigate the Windows Store to download applications tailored to your needs.

Beyond the fundamentals, we will guide you through the various productivity tools and functionalities that make the Surface Pro 10 a productivity powerhouse. From Microsoft Office applications to cloud storage integration, you will learn how to enhance your workflow and stay organized, whether you're working on documents, presentations, or spreadsheets.

For the creative souls, we have dedicated chapters to unleash the artistic potential of the Surface Pro 10. You will discover the versatility of the Surface Pen, enabling you to sketch, draw, and annotate effortlessly. We will explore digital art applications, offering tips and tricks to help you bring your imagination to life on the vibrant touchscreen canvas.

Furthermore, we will delve into the multimedia capabilities of the Surface Pro 10, allowing you to enjoy your favorite movies, music, and games with stunning visuals and rich audio. We will guide you through the process of transferring and organizing your media files, as well as introduce you to various entertainment apps available on the device.

That's not all we will also delve into the world of AI-Powered Performance:

The Surface Pro 10 is equipped with AI capabilities that go beyond traditional computing. Powered by the latest generation Intel Core Ultra processors featuring dedicated Neural Processing Units (NPUs), this device can intelligently optimize performance based on your usage patterns. From smoother multitasking to faster response times, AI ensures that your Surface Pro 10 adapts to your needs effortlessly.

By the end of this book, you will have gained the essential knowledge needed to harness the full potential of your Surface Pro 10. Whether you're a beginner or someone looking to optimize their experience, this guide aims to empower you with the skills and confidence to make the Surface Pro 10 an indispensable tool in your daily life.

So, let's embark on this exciting journey together, and unlock the endless possibilities that await you with the Microsoft Surface Pro 10!

**Microsoft introduces the Surface Pro 10 and Laptop 6, boasting advanced AI functionalities. Here's the scoop:**

Microsoft has introduced two new Surface devices, namely the Surface Pro 10 and the Surface Laptop 6. These devices mark Microsoft's first foray into hardware since the advent of the AI PC era, which began with Intel's and AMD's NPU-equipped chipsets.

Both models feature the new Intel Core Ultra (5 or 7) processor at their core. Microsoft highlights that the Surface Laptop 6 offers 2x the performance of its predecessor, the Laptop 5, while the Surface Pro 10 boasts a speed increase of up to 53% compared to the Pro 9. The inclusion of a dedicated Neural Processing Unit in the new chipsets enhances performance and efficiency, resulting in improved battery life, particularly for AI-related tasks like Windows Studio Effects, Live Captions, and productivity tools.

In terms of hardware enhancements, both devices feature a new anti-reflective coating that, when combined with brighter displays

(600 nits on the Surface Pro 10 and 400 nits on the Surface Laptop 6), enhances screen quality and viewing angles.

For enhanced security, the 15-inch version of the Surface Laptop 6 offers an integrated smart card reader, while the Surface Pro 10 includes an NFC reader to support security keys and other password less authentication tools.

The Surface Pro 10 boasts a new ultrawide, 10.5MP webcam capable of recording at 1440p resolution with a 114-degree field of view, surpassing the previous model's 1080p sensors.

Thanks to the efficiency gains from the Intel Core Ultra processors, Microsoft claims that both the Surface Pro 10 and Laptop 6 offer longer battery life compared to their predecessors. The Surface Pro 10 now lasts up to 19 hours (up from 15), while the Surface Laptop 6 offers a battery life of up to 19 hours (up from 17).

Microsoft has also made improvements in terms of repairability and serviceability, with QR codes on internal components for easier sourcing and visual indicators to identify screws and driver types.

Both models now come with 64GB of LPDDR5x RAM (previously limited to 32GB). The Surface Pro 10 starts with a base storage of 256GB instead of 128GB. The Surface Laptop 6 is available in 13.5-inch and 15-inch sizes. Pricing starts from $1,199, and both devices will be available for shipping on April 9.

Additionally, Microsoft is introducing 5G support for the Intel-equipped Surface Pro, a feature previously limited to devices powered by Qualcomm's SQ3 processor. The company is also offering Adaptive Accessories for commercial customers for the first time.

## Five biggest Microsoft's March Surface and AI event

Microsoft, a leading player in the field of artificial intelligence (AI), continues to innovate and introduce new offerings and updates to maintain its position at the forefront of the industry. To showcase its latest advancements, Microsoft recently held a Surface and Windows AI event in March, where it unveiled several new AI features and hardware.

The event primarily catered to Microsoft's enterprise customers, emphasizing the company's commitment to advancing the new era of work with its AI solutions. It is worth noting that Microsoft Build, scheduled for May, will likely feature announcements that are more relevant to general consumers. However, let's take a closer look at everything Microsoft revealed during its Surface event this week.

## 1. Microsoft 365's Copilot Arrives on Windows

A standout announcement from the event is the integration of Copilot capabilities from Microsoft 365 onto the Windows platform. This marks a significant advancement for professionals, as they can now access Copilot within the Windows interface. By selecting the "Work" option, users can enable Copilot in Microsoft 365 directly within Windows, as depicted in the image above.

The introduction of Copilot in Microsoft 365 on Windows represents a transformative shift in workflow management. This

7

feature seamlessly extends Copilot assistance to various 365 applications like Word, Excel, PowerPoint, Outlook, and more. It aids users in tasks ranging from crafting presentations to refining written content and interpreting spreadsheet data. Essentially, Copilot comprehends the entirety of the user's work ecosystem, offering enhanced assistance across the board.

**2. New Copilot accessibility features in Windows 11**

In an upcoming release of the Windows 11 preview by the month's end, users can anticipate a slew of new Copilot features geared towards accessibility. Among these enhancements, users will have the capability to request Copilot assistance for activating the narrator and screen magnifier, adjusting text size, and initiating live captions.

Empowering users to leverage Copilot for modifying PC settings provides a heightened level of control over their devices. This facilitates easier access to critical settings, eliminating the need to navigate through multiple tabs and simplifying the search for specific adjustments.

## 3. Introduction of AI-Powered Surface PCs for Business

Following the launch of the Surface Pro 9 and Surface Laptop 5 two years ago, Microsoft has unveiled their successors – the Surface Pro 10 and Surface Laptop 6. Positioned as Microsoft's inaugural hardware release in the AI PC era, these business-oriented devices have undergone significant upgrades, including a new processor optimized to bolster AI capabilities and productivity tasks.

Both models feature the latest Intel Core Ultra processors (5 or 7), incorporating a dedicated Neural Processing Unit (NPU) to enhance device performance and battery efficiency, particularly during AI-driven operations. Despite the under-the-hood improvements, the external appearance of the Surface devices remains largely unchanged, as illustrated in the accompanying image.

## 4. Windows 365 GPU Support

While not directly leveraging AI, the introduction of Windows 365 GPU support holds immense potential for streamlining professional workflows. This feature enables users to access GPU-enabled cloud PCs, offering enhanced graphics performance essential for demanding tasks like graphic design, image and video editing (including rendering), and more.

Microsoft's preview of Windows 365 GPU support responds to customer demands for GPU access within a Software-as-a-Service solution, promising to significantly enhance user experiences across various industries.

## 5. The first Copilot key on a Microsoft device

No AI PC launch would be complete without the mention of a dedicated Copilot key. Both the latest Surface devices and the new Surface Pro Keyboard, showcased in the accompanying image, now incorporate a designated Copilot key. This intuitive addition simplifies access to AI assistance for users. Furthermore, Windows users lacking the latest PC or Surface device can still access Copilot via the Copilot icon on the Windows 11 taskbar.

# How to Customize Your surface pro Keyboard in Windows 11

Utilize Microsoft PowerToys to Reassign Keys and Modify Keyboard Shortcuts

**Key Points to Note:**

1. Begin by downloading Microsoft PowerToys, then launch the application and navigate to Keyboard Manager > Remap a Key or Remap a Shortcut.

2. To revert keys and shortcuts to their default settings, simply click on the Trashcan icon adjacent to the respective entry.

3. For users with external keyboards and mice, the Windows Mouse and Keyboard Center tool offers customization options for both peripherals.

This comprehensive guide elucidates the process of keyboard customization in Windows 11. The instructions provided are applicable to both external keyboards and the integrated keyboards found in Windows-based laptops.

# How to Alter Keyboard Layout in Windows 11

The most straightforward method to tailor your keyboard experience is through PowerToys, a complimentary software developed by Microsoft. This tool empowers users to reassign keys and modify keyboard shortcuts via an intuitive interface. Additionally, PowerToys facilitates personalization of the operating system's layout and appearance.

**Follow these steps to reassign keys in Windows 11:**

1. Download Microsoft PowerToys and proceed with the installation on your PC.

2. Launch PowerToys and select Keyboard Manager from the sidebar menu.

3. Choose the option to Remap a Key.

If the keyboard settings appear grayed out, toggle the Enable Keyboard Manager switch.

4. Click on the Plus (+) symbol under Key.

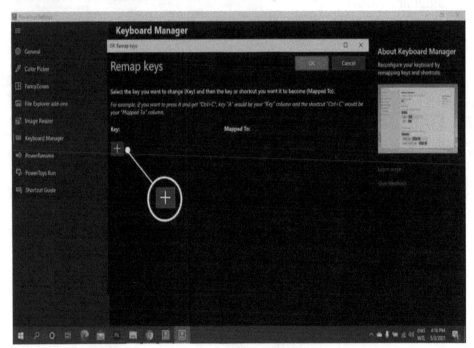

5. Select the desired key from the drop-down menu under Key, or opt to manually input a key by choosing Type.

6. Under Mapped To, designate the new key. To swap two keys, repeat steps 5 and 6 to create a corresponding entry, interchanging the keys accordingly.

Pro Tips: To restore a key to its default function, revisit this menu and click on the Trashcan icon next to the entry.

7. Confirm your selections by clicking OK.

If prompted with a notification indicating that the keys will no longer serve their original functions, proceed by selecting Continue Anyway.

## How to Customize Windows 11 Shortcuts in surface pro

Customizing keyboard shortcuts can be tailored for specific applications or system-wide adjustments:

1. Open Microsoft PowerToys and navigate to Keyboard Manager in the sidebar, then select Remap a Shortcut.

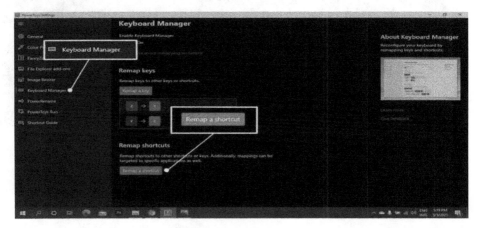

2. Click on the Plus (+) symbol under Shortcut.

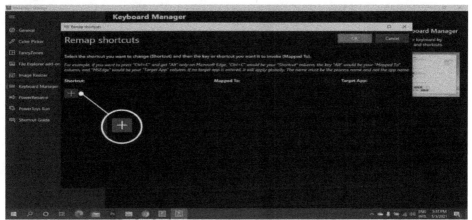

3. Choose the desired key from the dropdown menu or manually input a keyboard shortcut under Shortcut.

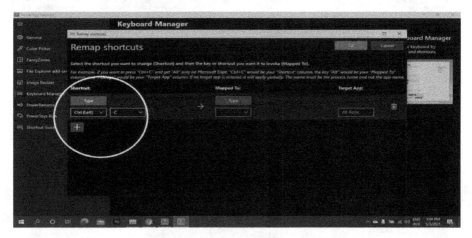

4. Under Mapped To, specify the new key or shortcut.

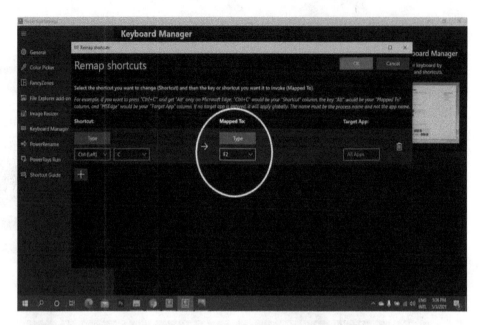

5. Optionally, specify Target Apps by entering the name of the relevant application. Leaving this field blank will apply the changes system-wide.

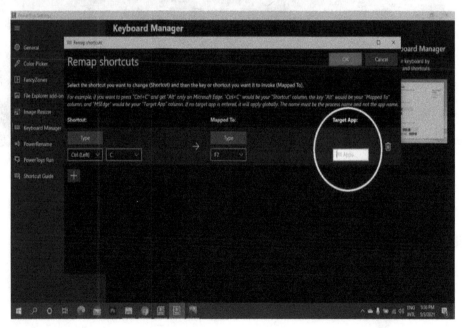

# 6. Confirm your alterations by clicking OK.

# How to set Up Microsoft Surface Device

The Windows setup process will commence automatically for new Surface devices or those that have been reset since their last use. Here's a walkthrough:

Upon startup, the setup tool will prompt you to select your region. Confirm the correct region or select the appropriate one from the list provided.

Verify if the suggested keyboard layout is correct. If not, choose the correct layout from the options presented.

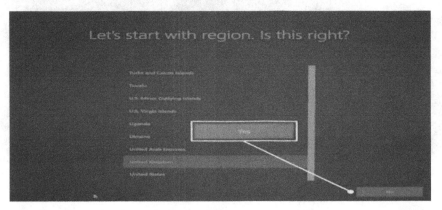

If prompted to add a second keyboard layout, proceed accordingly. Most users can skip this step unless using keyboards for different languages.

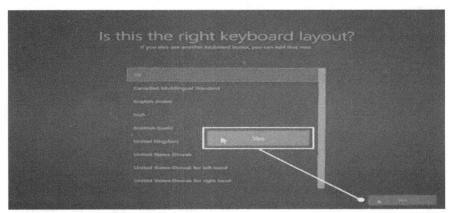

Follow the on-screen instructions to pair a Surface Pen if one was included with your device. You can opt to do this later if preferred.

Connect to a Wi-Fi network by selecting it from the available options and entering the password.

Review and accept the license agreement by tapping Accept.

Choose the setup option based on personal or enterprise use. For personal devices, select Set up for personal use.

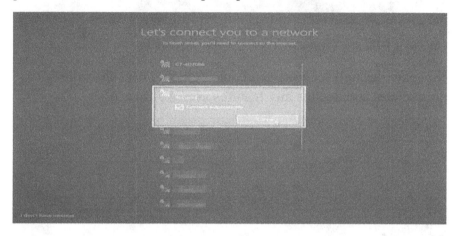

Enter your Microsoft account email and password to proceed with the setup.

Note: A Microsoft account is mandatory for setup unless a Wi-Fi network wasn't selected earlier.

If your Surface device supports Windows Hello facial recognition login, follow the prompts to set it up.

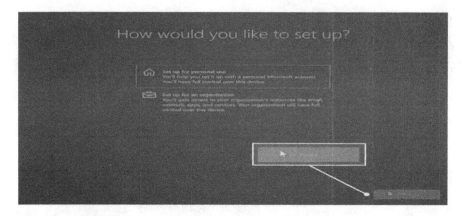

Create a PIN for your device when prompted.

Navigate through successive menus regarding data sharing preferences and decline any features you're unsure of.

Decide whether to back up files to OneDrive or skip this step.

9. Acknowledge any reminders regarding installed Office apps, if applicable.

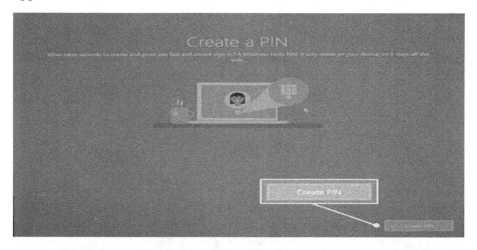

Optionally, set up Cortana or skip this step if not interested.

Decline additional offers or subscriptions as per your preference.

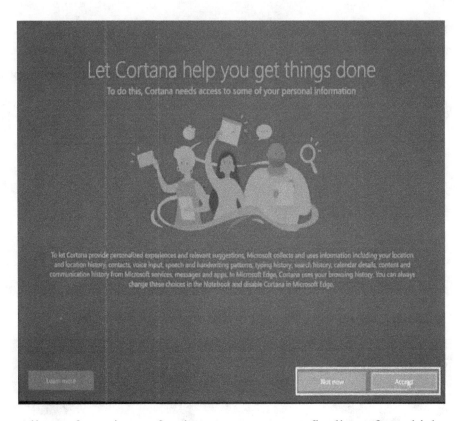

Allow a few minutes for the setup process to finalize, after which the Windows desktop will appear.

.

# Major Things That You Must Know About the Microsoft Surface Pro 10 2024.

**Key Highlights of the Microsoft Surface Pro 10 (2024)**

## 1. Advanced Performance:

The Surface Pro 10 boasts enhanced performance capabilities compared to its predecessors, powered by the latest generation Intel Core Ultra processors (5 or 7). This ensures smoother multitasking and improved efficiency, making it an ideal choice for professionals handling demanding tasks.

## 2. AI Integration:

Embracing the era of AI-powered computing, the Surface Pro 10 integrates AI functionalities to augment productivity. With a dedicated Neural Processing Unit (NPU), users can expect accelerated performance, particularly in AI-driven applications and tasks.

## 3. Sleek and Functional Design:

Continuing the Surface Pro legacy, the Surface Pro 10 maintains its signature sleek and versatile design. Whether used as a tablet or paired with a detachable keyboard for a laptop-like experience, its form factor remains both stylish and functional.

## 4. Enhanced Connectivity:

Equipped with advanced connectivity options, including Wi-Fi 6E support, users can experience faster and more reliable wireless connections. This ensures seamless access to online resources and improved productivity, even in bandwidth-intensive environments.

## 5. Innovative Input Methods:

The Surface Pro 10 introduces innovative input methods to streamline user interaction. With the inclusion of a dedicated Copilot key on the device and compatible Surface Pro keyboards, accessing AI assistance is more intuitive than ever, offering users immediate access to productivity-enhancing features.

## 6. Immersive Display and Audio:

Featuring a vibrant high-resolution display and immersive audio capabilities, the Surface Pro 10 offers an unparalleled multimedia experience. Whether presenting visuals or consuming content, users can enjoy crisp visuals and rich sound quality, enhancing both work and entertainment activities.

## 7. Enhanced Security Features:

With an emphasis on data security, the Surface Pro 10 integrates advanced security features to safeguard user information and privacy. From biometric authentication methods such as Windows Hello facial recognition to robust encryption protocols, users can trust their device to protect sensitive data.

**8. Eco-Friendly Construction:**

Microsoft's commitment to sustainability is reflected in the Surface Pro 10's eco-friendly construction. Utilizing recycled materials and adhering to stringent environmental standards, the device minimizes its carbon footprint without compromising performance or durability.

**9. Seamless Integration with Microsoft Ecosystem:**

As part of the Microsoft ecosystem, the Surface Pro 10 seamlessly integrates with Microsoft 365 and other productivity tools. This ensures compatibility and interoperability across platforms, allowing users to transition seamlessly between devices and applications.

**10. Comprehensive Support and Warranty:**

Backed by Microsoft's comprehensive support and warranty services, Surface Pro 10 users can rely on prompt assistance and coverage for hardware issues. This peace of mind enhances the overall ownership experience, ensuring continued satisfaction and productivity.

These key features collectively position the Microsoft Surface Pro 10 as a versatile and powerful computing device, catering to the diverse needs of modern professionals in 2024 and beyond.

11. You can use Microsoft's new Surface Slim Pen 2 with the tablet, offering an enhanced digital pen experience that's known for its realism and lifelike feel, a feature not available in Surface 9.

12. The Microsoft Surface Pro 10 operates on Windows 11 for home users and Windows 11 Pro for commercial users.

13. The Surface Pro 10 boasts a front-facing camera with IR capabilities at 5 megapixels (1440p), and a rear-facing camera at 10 megapixels (1440p, 4K).

14. The Microsoft Surface Pro 10 includes a 5G model featuring the Qualcomm Snapdragon 8cx G3 (Microsoft SQ3) ARM chip.

# Sign In with A Microsoft Account

To begin, you'll need an email address. Once you have one, you can access the following features:

- Unlimited online storage

- An online option to change your Surface password.

- With a Microsoft account, you can unlock many additional capabilities.

## Registering Your Surface To A Microsoft Account

By connecting your Surface to a Microsoft account, you'll be able to easily manage your device's warranty details and access technical support from anywhere you are. Signing in with your Microsoft account offers several advantages:

# Benefits Of Using Your Microsoft Account:

- Link your device to yourself using your Microsoft account. With a free Microsoft account, you can effortlessly access all your digital content and synchronize everything you need across your device.

- Gain access to Office Online, Skype, Outlook, OneDrive, OneNote, and various other applications for free.

- Explore more entertainment options through the Microsoft Store and Xbox Live, customized to match your interests.

- Easily access your favorite games, apps, movies, music, and more by signing in with Microsoft.

- Stay connected with loved ones using Skype for HD video calls and messaging, and manage your inbox with ease using Outlook.

- Enjoy consistent account settings across all your devices, ensuring your important documents and files are always within reach.

- Shop securely, back up your files in the cloud, and access additional privacy options.

- Earn points with every Microsoft purchase or search, which can be redeemed for movies, gift cards, games, music, or charitable donations.

# How To Get Your Surface Pro 10 Registration Done

By registering your Surface device, you can easily monitor your warranty status and receive prompt technical assistance. Additionally, you'll have access to the following benefits:

- Receive assistance with hardware issues.
- Utilize chat or phone support for assistance.
- Monitor the status of service requests or cancel them if needed.

To register your Microsoft Surface device, follow these steps:

1. Visit the registration page by clicking on this link: (https://devicesupport.microsoft.com). If you're already signed in, your profile name and icon will appear in the top right corner of the page.

2. If you're not signed in, click on "Sign In" in the top right corner and enter your Microsoft account information. If you don't have a Microsoft account yet, you can create one by selecting the "Sign Up" option. You need a Microsoft account to register your device.

3. Once signed in, you'll return to the Device Support page, where you can access device registration, warranty information, and the service page.

4. In the Overview section, next to "My Devices," click on "Register my device" to begin the registration process.

5. If you haven't registered any devices, navigate to "My Devices" and click on the blue "Get Started" button to initiate the registration process.

6. A page titled "Register your Microsoft Device" will appear.

7. Select your country or region from the provided list.

8. Choose your product family type from the dropdown menu.

9. On the Registration page, enter your serial number in the designated box.

10. Check the box to indicate your agreement with the privacy statement.

11. Click the blue "Register" button. Once your device is successfully registered, you'll receive a confirmation message stating, "Success! You have successfully registered your device."

12. Click on "Device Support" at the top of the page to view and manage your registered device.

# Type Cover and Keyboard in Surface Pro 10

You can use your Surface Pro 10 with an additional Type Cover. Remember, both Bluetooth and USB keyboards will function seamlessly with your Surface.

1. To attach your Type Cover, simply click it onto the bottom of your Surface.

2. To remove the Type Cover, gently pull it away from your Surface.

## Charger

The Surface device charger consists of two components:

- Power brick
- Power supply cord

The power brick features a USB port that allows you to charge other devices. It's worth noting that the Surface Pro m3 charger and all Surface Go chargers lack an additional USB charging port.

It's important to handle power cords with care, as they can easily break if twisted or bent excessively in the same spot. Here are some crucial steps to ensure the safety of your power cord:

- Regularly inspect your power cord, particularly where it connects to the power brick.
- Avoid twisting or pinching the power cord.
- When wrapping the power cord around the power brick, use loose coils.
- Properly wrap your cables to prevent damage.
- Remember to wrap cables loosely, as demonstrated in the image below:
- Avoid tightly wrapping cables like this.

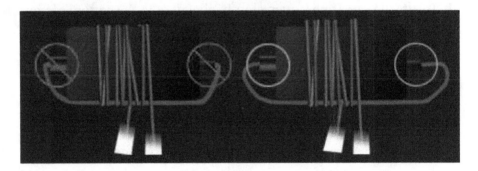

# Chapter 1:

# Configuration of Surface Mobile Mouse with Microsoft Mouse and Keyboard Center

Don't miss out on these useful tips for optimizing your mouse settings. You can adjust the DPI value, right and left click functions, scrolling behavior, and wheel button click on the Surface Mobile Mouse.

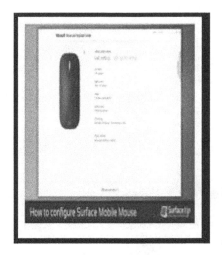

The Microsoft Surface Mobile Mouse is highly regarded for its sleek appearance, affordability, slim design, and ambidextrous shape, catering to both left and right-handed users. It comes in platinum, cobalt blue, and burgundy colors, as well as three quality tone-on-tone options. The scroll wheel has been improved for better accuracy and comfort, featuring a new metal design.

A standout feature of the Microsoft Surface Mobile Mouse is its easy customization, particularly through "button remapping." This feature ensures that both right-handed and left-handed users can enjoy the same experience. To access this feature, you'll need to install the Microsoft Surface Mobile Mouse and Keyboard Center on your computer. In this guide, we'll walk you through the process of adjusting right and left click functions, wheel button presses, and DPI settings.

**1.      Configuring The Surface Mobile Mouse With Microsoft Mouse And Keyboard Center**

Ensure the following steps are completed to set up your Surface Mobile Mouse:

1. Download and install the Microsoft Mouse and Keyboard Center on your computer. You can learn how to download and set up the Microsoft Mouse and Keyboard Center here.

2. Connect the Surface Mobile Mouse to your computer. You can find instructions on how to link a Surface Mobile Mouse to your PC here.

3. Once connected, access the Microsoft Mouse and Keyboard Center through the Start menu. If done correctly, the Surface Mobile Mouse settings interface will appear like this:

Now you're ready to get started. Continue reading to learn more about your Surface Mobile Mouse.

## 2. Changing What The Surface Mobile Mouse's Left Button Does

One of the standout features of the Surface Mobile Mouse is its ability to switch between right and left clicks. You can easily do this by pressing the Action key on the Surface Mobile Mouse to alter the function of the left button.

1. Start by selecting the Left button option on the main setup page.

2. You'll then be directed to the settings page for the left button.

On the "Left button" settings page, you have the option to customize how the "Left button" functions by adjusting the following settings:

- Keep the default click action as it is.
- Change the right-click function, allowing left-handed individuals to right-click effortlessly.

**3.     Reprogramming the Surface Mobile Mouse's right button**

If you need to switch from right-click to left-click on the Surface Mobile Mouse, you can easily do so. Here's how to change the function of your right-click button:

1. Start by selecting the "Right" button option on the main setup page.

2. You'll then be directed to the settings page for the right button.

On the "Right Button" settings page, you have the option to customize how the "Right button" functions by adjusting the following settings:

- Keep the default click action unchanged.
- Adjust the right-click function to enable left-handed individuals to click it with their left hand.

**4. Setting Up How The Scrolling Works On The Surface Mobile Mouse**

In the Microsoft Mouse and Keyboard Center, you have the option to customize how the Surface Mobile Mouse functions when scrolling. Here's how to do it:

1. Navigate to the setup page and select "Wheel."

2. You'll be directed to a page where you can adjust the wheel settings.

On this configuration page, you can enable or disable various scrolling features and adjust their values:

- Enable or disable vertical scrolling using a two-finger swipe up or down, and adjust the scrolling speed.

- Enable accelerated vertical scrolling, which allows you to navigate through documents or web pages faster, viewing more content at once. This is particularly useful when scrolling through lengthy documents or web pages.

- Toggle the scrolling direction to change the way you scroll up and down.

## Setting Up The Surface Mobile Mouse "Wheel Button Click"

In the Microsoft Mouse and Keyboard Center, you can customize the function of the wheel button to perform specific actions. Here's how:

1. Navigate to the setup page and select the "Wheel button."

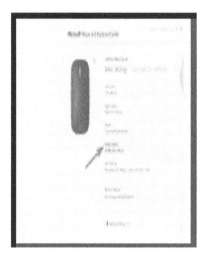

2. You'll be directed to a page where you can adjust the settings for the wheel button.

On the Surface Mobile Mouse, the "wheel button click" can be configured to perform one of six different actions:

1. Middle click (default) - Utilize the default action associated with middle-clicking (also known as "scroll wheel click").

2. Choose a key combination - Select a manual key combination for the wheel button click.

3. Macros - Create a series of events, such as mouse clicks, keystrokes, and time delays, to assist with repetitive tasks or sequences. Once a macro is created, it can be assigned to a button or the mouse for easy execution.

4. View all commands - Assign the wheel button click to one of the available commands listed.

5. Disable this button - Turn off the wheel button functionality.

Examples of pre-set commands that can be assigned are available for selection.

**Windows commands**

Here are various actions you can assign to the wheel button click in the Microsoft Mouse and Keyboard Center:

Desktop Actions:

- Task View
- Add New Desktop
- Previous Desktop
- Next Desktop
- Close Desktop

**Window Management:**

- Snap Windows Left
- Snap Windows Right
- Snap Windows Up
- Snap Windows Down
- Open Action Center
- Open Cortana
- Show/Hide App Commands
- Search
- Connect
- Settings

- Go to Windows Start

- Close

- Exit Program

- Show/Hide Desktop

- Next Window

- Previous Window

**Browser Commands:**

- Browser Back

- Browser Forward

**Content Commands:**

- Copy (Ctrl+C)

- Cut (Ctrl+X)

- Delete

- Paste (Ctrl+V)

- Undo (Ctrl+Z)

- Redo (Ctrl+Y)

- Page Up

- Page Down

- Print Screen

## Document Commands:

- New
- Open

## Key Commands:

- Alt
- Ctrl
- Shift
- Enter

**Configuring the DPI settings on Surface Mobile Mouse**

For the Surface Mobile Mouse, you have the option to customize the DPI (dots per linear inch) value to suit your preferences and environment. Here's how to do it:

1. Navigate to the main settings page and select the DPI settings.

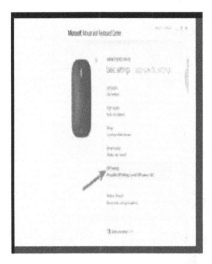

2. You'll be directed to a page where you can adjust your DPI settings.

On this configuration page, you can input a number between 400 and 1800. Make sure to test it out immediately to ensure it works well for you.

**Putting The Surface Mobile Mouse Back To Its Original Settings**

If you've made changes and need to revert to the original settings, follow these steps:

1. After making alterations from the default settings, you'll notice a new option on the configuration page labeled "Restore Default." Click on this option to proceed.

2. You'll then see two additional buttons. Press "Restore" to revert everything back to its original state.

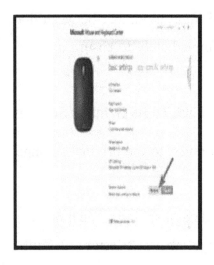

# CHAPTER 2:

# HOW TO WORK ON THE GO WITH YOUR SURFACE PRO 10 DEVICE

## Absence Of Wi-Fi

If you're in an area without Wi-Fi, there's no need to fret. With a Surface Pro 10 equipped with LTE Advanced, such as the Surface Pro or Surface Go, you can easily insert your mobile service SIM card to access the internet wherever there's a cellular signal.

Depending on your mobile provider, data usage may incur charges. Feel free to inquire with your cell phone company for more details on how it works.

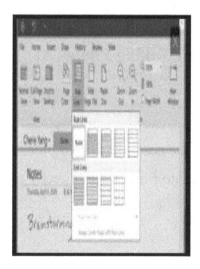

## Using Your Surface Pro 10 As A Notebook

If you find yourself without a physical notebook, your Surface Pro 10 can serve as a digital alternative. You can write notes in OneNote using your digital pen, providing a similar experience to writing in a traditional notebook.

Moreover, once you start jotting down notes in OneNote with the digital pen, all your notes will be automatically saved in OneDrive, ensuring you don't lose any crucial information. To add lines or grids to your notes, simply open OneNote, click on View, and then select Rule Lines.

## Signing And Sending Contracts

Instead of faxing contracts, you can conveniently open them on your Surface device, sign them using the Surface pen, and then email the file for processing.

## Using Your Surface Device For Taking Photos At Work

With the Camera app on your Surface device, you can effortlessly capture photos and make edits without the need to use your phone. These photos can then be incorporated into files or sent directly to your colleagues.

Here's how to take photos:

1. Open the Camera app.

2. Capture a photo.

3. Select the photo from your camera roll.

4. Choose "Edit & Create."

5. Opt for "Draw" and utilize your Surface pen to add notes.

6. Click on "Save a copy."

# Turning A Screen Into A Wireless Display

Here's a simplified guide to performing various tasks with your Surface device:

## Setting Up Wireless Display:

I.      Turn on your monitor and connect the wireless display adapter.

II.     Access the Action Center.

III.    Choose "Project."

IV.     Select the name that matches your computer screen.

## Clicking Through A Slideshow:

I.      Utilize the digital pen as a clicker during PowerPoint presentations.

II.     Press the eraser button to advance to the next slide.

III.    Press and hold the eraser button to move back a slide.

## Instantly Sharing Files With People:

I.      Navigate to the Action Center.

II.     Enable "Share with people nearby."

III. Access File Explorer.

IV. Choose the desired file.

V. Click on "Share."

VI. Select a PC to send the file copy.

## Using Onedrive To Collaborate:

I. Open File Explorer.

II. Click on "OneDrive."

III. Drag a file into the window and right-click it.

IV. Click on "More OneDrive sharing options" to involve everyone.

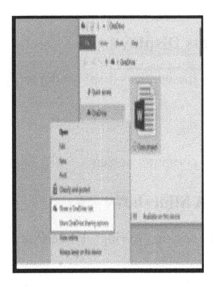

## Managing All Your Mail Accounts In Outlook

You can easily manage all your email accounts, including Yahoo! Mail, Gmail, Hotmail, etc., using Outlook on your Surface or phone. Here's how to set it up:

1. Download the Outlook app.

2. Navigate to the "Home" section in the menu.

3. Click on "Settings."

4. Select the "Add Account" link.

5. Click the "Add Email Account" button to proceed.

Ensuring Your Voice is Heard:

1. Open the document in Excel, Word, or PowerPoint.

2. Go to the "Review" tab.

3. Click on "Add New Comment."

4. Type the person's name followed by @.

5. Share your thoughts or feedback.

If done correctly, an email notification will be automatically sent to the designated person.

## Giving Feedback With The Use Of Surface Pen

You can easily edit and annotate Excel, Word, and PowerPoint documents using the Surface Pen. Here's how you can do it:

1. Open the document you want to edit in Excel, Word, or PowerPoint.

2. Navigate to the "Draw" menu, which provides a convenient way to add annotations and feedback.

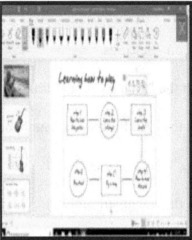

## Adding 3D Objects To Your Office Files:

1. Open Excel, Word, PowerPoint, or Outlook.

2. Click on "Insert."

3. Select "3D Models."

4. Choose "From a File" to upload a 3D model saved on your device.

5. Alternatively, select "From Online Sources" to browse and find a 3D model available online.

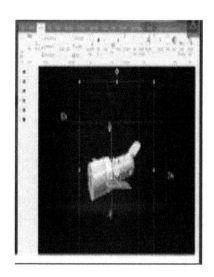

## Animate 3D Models In Powerpoint

1. Open the presentation you want to work on.

2. To insert a 3D model, go to the "Insert" tab and select "3D Models" from the dropdown menu.

3. Duplicate the slide you want to work on.

4. Click on the 3D model added to the second slide.

5. Adjust its position, then navigate to the "Transitions" tab and choose "Morph."

6. Navigating Slideshows with a Mouse

7. When presenting in PowerPoint, you can use the digital pen as a clicker.

8. Simply press the button resembling an eraser to proceed to the next slide.

9. Press and hold the same button to move back to the previous slide.

## Writing In Full-Screen Mode

To minimize distractions while writing, follow these steps:

i. Launch OneNote.

ii. Click on the "Enter Full Screen Mode" option.

iii. Use your Surface Pen to write and draw, just like you would with a traditional notebook.

## Doing The Math With Onenote

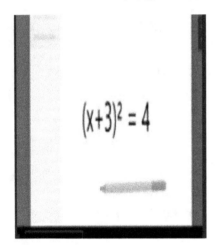

i. With the Surface Pen, you can write out an equation.

ii. Select the "Draw" option.

iii. Use the "Lasso Select" tool to circle the equation.

iv. Select "Mathematics."

v. Tap the action button, and OneNote will handle the rest.

# Using Handwriting To Convert Text

Follow these steps to transfer notes from OneNote:

i. Go to the "Draw" tab.

ii. Select "Lasso Select."

iii. Draw a circle around the handwritten text.

iv. Choose "Ink to text," and it will be ready to copy and paste.

# CHAPTER 3:

# HOW TO ENABLE HIBERNATION SUPPORT ON 2024 SURFACE PRO 10

Microsoft recently updated all Surface devices with a new feature called modern standby. This means that hibernation is now turned off by default. With modern standby, your device can switch on and off instantly, perform tasks in the background while it's off, and use a simpler wake-up process.

While modern standby lets you resume your work immediately, it does use some battery power. If you're not planning to use your Surface for a while, it's a good idea to put it into hibernation to conserve battery.

In this guide, I'll explain how to put your Surface into hibernation right from the power menu in the Start menu.

## How To Check The Hibernate Option In System Power Settings

To see if your Surface is set to hibernate, follow these steps:

- Right-click on the battery icon in the system tray.
- Choose Power Options.
- Click on "Choose what the power buttons do."

- Under Shutdown settings, check if there's an option for Hibernate. If not, hibernation is currently disabled.

## Enabling Hibernation Support Via Command Line Or Powershell

To turn on hibernation support for your Surface, do the following:

- Right-click the "Start" button.
- Select Windows PowerShell (Admin).
- Type "powercfg /h on" and hit Enter in Windows PowerShell.
- Go back to Power Options > System Settings, and you should now see the Hibernate option under Shutdown settings.
- You can now put your Surface into hibernation directly from the power menu in the Start menu.

# CHAPTER 4:

# SURFACE PRO 10 AND YOUR PHONE

Ensure smooth compatibility between your phone and PC across applications like OneNote, Word, PowerPoint, Excel, and others. These Office applications are available for Macs, iPads, Android phones, and Android tablets.

## Improving Internet Speed

Enhance your Surface Go's internet speed by connecting it to Ethernet using the Surface USB-C to Ethernet adapter while you're working at your desk. Simply plug one end of an Ethernet cable into your Surface Go and the other into your router.

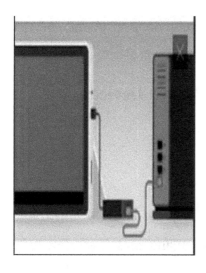

Enhancing Your Phone with Microsoft Features

1. Open the Google Play Store on your phone.

2. Search for "Microsoft launcher" and install it.

3. Once installed, enjoy daily changing Bing wallpapers and sync your Office documents, calendar, and more.

## Customizing Your Feed

1. Swipe left from your home screen.

2. Select "More."

3. Choose "Customize feed" to arrange events, news, documents, sticky notes, calendars, and more to your liking.

## Using Sticky Notes On PC And Android

1. Open Sticky Notes on your PC and go to Settings.

2. Sign in with your Microsoft account to sync your notes.

3. Access your notes from the home screen on your phone and tap to open.

## Accessing Documents Across Devices

1. Launch Microsoft Word on your computer.

2. Sign in with your Microsoft account.

3. Create a new document.

4. Swipe across your phone's home screen and click "Timeline."

5. Open the file from there.

## Getting Microsoft Edge On Your Phone

Microsoft Edge allows seamless browsing between your Windows 10 PC and your phone or tablet. Your data syncs automatically across all your devices.

## Sending Webpages From Phone To PC

Connect your phone to your computer and choose "Continue on PC" to easily send a webpage from your phone.

## Getting Access To Your Favorites And Many More On Your Phone

Starting with Microsoft Edge:

1. Open Microsoft Edge.

2. Click on "Settings and more."

3. Sign in with your Microsoft account to sync your favorites and other preferences to your computer.

## Accessing Emails Easily:

You can conveniently check your emails from anywhere using Microsoft Outlook Mobile. Simply set up the same email account you use on your computer, and you'll be able to access all your emails on the go, right from your device.

## Adding Pictures To Your Phone And Surface:

1. Launch the OneDrive app on your phone.

2. Sign in using your Microsoft account.

3. Check that "Camera Upload" is enabled in the app settings.

4. On your Surface, locate the OneDrive icon on the right side of the taskbar.

5. Open the OneDrive folder.

6. Navigate to the folder containing your camera roll to view your pictures.

# CHAPTER 5:

# HOW TO SET CUSTOM SCREEN RESOLUTIONS ON MICROSOFT SURFACE PRO 10

The Microsoft Surface comes with a high-resolution screen filled with millions of pixels, ensuring sharp clarity for users. However, this feature can sometimes lead to issues, particularly when using software or older applications that aren't optimized for display scaling.

To address this, software developers must update their programs to work seamlessly with high DPI displays, resolving any scaling problems that may arise. Alternatively, users can adjust their Surface display's resolution and scaling to 100% to mitigate these issues. It's worth noting that Windows 10 lacks 3:2 resolution options beyond the default maximum resolution on the Surface.

Why Custom Resolutions for Microsoft Surface?

### 2024 Surface Pro 10 Screen Resolution

The Surface Pro 10 boasts a 13-inch touch display called "PixelSense Flow" with impressive specifications. It offers a resolution of 2,880 x 1,920 pixels, a 3:2 aspect ratio, and a high refresh rate of 120Hz. The display is equipped with anti-reflective technology, ensuring optimal visibility even in challenging lighting conditions. Additionally, the adaptive color feature enhances the screen's visual quality, guaranteeing an excellent viewing experience.

There are situations where a unique solution is needed. Here are a few examples:

1. When you're using software that doesn't support high DPI displays.

2. When troubleshooting issues with multiple screens having different scaling settings.

3. When optimizing your gaming experience, lower resolution and a 3:2 aspect ratio can be beneficial.

## Microsoft Surface Screen Resolution

To add a custom resolution to your Surface, you may need to understand native resolution and resolution at 100% scaling.

## How To Add Custom Resolutions To The System Resolution List?

Here's how to do it using a tool called CRU (Custom Resolution Utility):

1. Obtain the CRU report (Custom Resolution Utility).

2. Open the downloaded file.

3. Launch the CRU tool.

4. Click "Add" under "Detailed Resolutions" to input a custom resolution.

5. Select the desired horizontal and vertical resolutions (e.g., 2880 width and 1920 height for Surface Pro 3).

6. Close the detailed resolution dialog box by clicking OK.

7. Confirm changes by clicking OK again.

8. Restart your computer to apply the changes.

## Applying Your New Custom Resolution:

After restarting, you can set your new custom resolution by following these steps:

1. Go to Settings, then System, and finally Display.

2. Choose your new resolution under Resolution (e.g., 2880 x 1920).

3. Click "Keep Changes" to apply your new resolution.

### Alternative Methods:

Besides using the CRU tool, you can utilize a predefined list of screen resolutions for Surface Pro 3, Surface Pro 4, and Surface Book with a regkey. This list includes 3:2 aspect ratios.

# CHAPTER 6:

# EDIT WORD DOCS USING THE SURFACE PEN

To manipulate text in Word using various drawing tools, follow these steps:

Circling Text to Select in Word:

1. Open a Word document.

2. Click on "Draw."

3. Select "Ink Editor."

4. Use the Surface Pen to draw a circle around a word or text fragment.

5. Now, you can cut, copy, or paste the selected text as needed.

## Crossing Out Words For Deletion In Word:

1. Start a Word document.

2. Click on "Draw."

3. Choose "Ink Editor."

4. Utilize the Surface Pen to delete words, paragraphs, or phrases by drawing a diagonal line through them.

# Joining Words With A Curve In Word:

1. Begin a Word document.

2. Click on "Draw."

3. Opt for "Ink Editor."

4. Use the Surface Pen to connect two words by drawing a curve between them, ensuring the curve's ends touch the words you intend to connect.

## Splitting Words With A Line In Word:

1. Open a Word document.

2. Select "Draw."

3. Choose "Ink Editor."

4. Employ the Surface Pen to draw a vertical line in the middle of a word to divide it into two parts.

## Inserting Words Using A Caret In Word:

1. Start a Word document.

2. Click on "Draw."

3. Select "Ink Editor."

4. Draw a caret between two words using the Surface Pen.

5. Type the text you wish to add, and it will be inserted automatically.

## Creating A New Line In Word:

1. Begin a Word document.

2. Choose "Draw."

3. Select "Ink Editor."

4. Use the Surface Pen to draw an inverted L shape. Text following this shape will start on a new line.

## Highlighting Text In Word:

1. Start a Word document.

2. Select "Draw."

3. Opt for "Ink Editor."

4. Click on "Highlighter."

5. Use your pen to mark the text you want to emphasize.

# Replaying Pen Strokes In Word

To review a sequence of actions you've taken in Word, follow these steps:

1. Begin a new Word document.

2. Click on "Draw."

3. Select "Replay in Ink."

# CHAPTER 7:

# HOW TO ENABLE BATTERY LIMIT FEATURE ON SURFACE PRO 10 DEVICES

Microsoft introduced a new feature called "Battery Limit" to all Surface devices, starting with the Surface Pro 3 in September 2018. This feature aims to prolong the battery life by restricting the charge to a maximum of 50%.

Enabling this feature preserves the battery's capacity to hold a charge, especially for Surface devices that remain connected to an external power source for extended periods, such as kiosks or game consoles. The feature is being rolled out to Surface devices through firmware updates.

## How To Enable The Battery Limit Feature On Compatible Surface Devices:

1. Put your Surface to sleep.

2. Press and hold the Volume Up button, then briefly press and release the Power button.

3. Release the Volume Up button when the Surface logo appears, and the Surface UEFI screen appears shortly after.

4. Select the Boot Configuration page from the Surface UEFI menu.

5. Under "Advanced Options," toggle the switch to enable "Battery Limit Mode."

6. After making changes, restart your Surface by accessing the Exit menu and selecting Restart Now.

## To Verify That The Battery Limit Feature Is Enabled:

Click on the battery icon in the Windows taskbar to open the battery status window. You'll observe that the battery stops charging at 50% after some time.

# CHAPTER 8:

# MAKE NOTES ON A WEB PAGE

Adding Notes on Microsoft Edge:

To add notes in Microsoft Edge, tap on "Settings and more," then select "More tools," and finally click on "Add Notes." You can write or draw anything you like and easily share it on social media or via email.

## Adding Notes To A Photo With Your Surface:

Share your thoughts about a photo by adding notes. Open the Camera app, take a photo, then select the image from your camera roll. Go to "Edit & Create" and click on "Draw." Use your Surface Pen to add notes, then click "Save a copy."

## Clearing Your Workspace:

Stay focused by closing all apps except the one you're using. Click and hold on the window you want to keep open, then gently shake your finger or mouse back and forth. Other open apps will automatically minimize, giving you more space.

## Writing In Full Screen Mode:

Eliminate distractions by writing in full-screen mode. Open OneNote, tap on "Enter Full Screen Mode," and use your Surface Pen to write or draw, just like you would in a notebook.

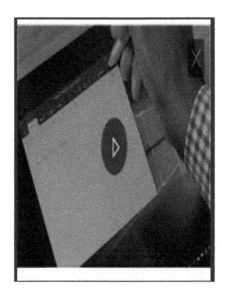

## Saving In A Sticky Note:

Organize your reminders with Sticky Notes. Open the Windows Ink Workspace and click on "Sticky Notes." Create a new note, then use the pen to jot down your reminder.

# CHAPTER 9:

# THE SURFACE PRO 10 APP

### Check Surface Accessory Power:

In the Surface app, you can easily monitor the remaining power of your Surface Pen or Mouse. Simply click on "Battery level" to view more details.

### Adjust Surface Pen Sensitivity:

Open the Surface app and navigate to the Pen settings. From there, you can customize the amount of Windows Ink displayed on the screen based on the pressure sensitivity of your pen.

## Find Your Surface Serial Number:

Easily locate your Surface's serial number and other information by tapping on your Surface within the Surface app. This feature makes it convenient to copy and paste the details as needed.

# Maximizing Microsoft Surface Battery Life:

Learn how to optimize your Microsoft Surface's battery life for various situations such as attending classes, meetings, or working remotely.

Battery life depends on two main factors: "battery capacity" and "power efficiency," which are inherent to the device. Check the Surface app to monitor your device's battery life.

This guide will demonstrate how to adjust power settings and system configurations on your Surface to extend battery life, including:

- Real-time monitoring of battery usage
- Optimization with Surface Pro Power Plan
- Adjusting Cortana settings
- Disabling Wi-Fi overnight
- Lowering screen brightness
- Managing startup applications
- Utilizing Microsoft Edge for web browsing
- Enabling battery saver mode
- Turning off Bluetooth radio

Before diving into strategies to prolong battery life on Surface Pro 4 and Surface Book, it's essential to monitor the current battery drain rate. Observing the rate of battery depletion allows us to understand:

# How Much Power Is Used In The Whole System In Real-Time?

**Monitoring Real-Time Power Usage:**

Have you ever wondered how much power your system consumes in real-time? Certain activities can drain power more quickly than others. By adjusting your system settings, you can observe the power usage.

**Utilizing Battery Bar:**

In my experience, Battery Bar proves to be the most effective tool for monitoring battery usage. It provides comprehensive real-time information about battery drain. Here are some key details it offers:

- Surface Pro 3 and Surface Pro 4 battery capacity comparison
- Current discharge rate, displayed in milliwatts (mW) and watts (W)
- Battery capacity percentage

**Interpreting Battery Information:**

For instance, my current discharge rate is 3,539 mW, which equals 3.5W, and my battery capacity is 82.9%. This indicates that, given my current system setup and activities, my battery can last approximately 6 hours and 16 minutes.

Understanding this, it becomes clear that to prolong battery life, it's crucial to minimize the discharge rate. Let's optimize the battery usage of your Surface Pro 4 to maximize its lifespan.

## Optimizing Surface Pro Power Settings

By default, Microsoft Surface devices come with a power plan named "Balanced," offering limited advanced settings.

### Step 1: Disabling Connected Standby

Since Connected Standby is enabled by default on all Surface devices, accessing advanced power settings can be restricted. To create a new power plan with enhanced settings, we'll use the Registry Editor to disable Connected Standby.

**To turn off Connected Standby:**

1. Press the Windows key + R on your keyboard.

2. Type "regedit" to open the Registry Editor.

3. Double-click on "CsEnabled," change the "Value" from "1" to "0," and click "OK."

4. Restart your computer to apply the changes.

5. After restarting, you'll have access to the complete list of power plans and their advanced settings.

**Reviewing Default Balanced Power Plan Settings**

Before proceeding to create the Surface Pro Optimization power plan, let's examine the settings of the default balanced power plan that we'll replicate for our new plan.

**Step 3: Creating the Surface Pro Optimization Power Plan**

To establish a power plan tailored for the Surface Pro based on the balanced power plan:

- Navigate to Start > Control Panel > Right-click.
- Go to Hardware and Sound > Power Options.
- On the left side, select "Create a power plan."
- Enter "Surface Pro Optimization" as the plan name (you can choose any other name).
- After creating the plan, click on "Change advanced power settings" to customize the settings.
- Adjust the settings as needed, ensuring they match those of the default balanced power plan.
- Once done, click OK to apply the changes.

**Important Note:**

Remember to revert the value of CsEnabled back to "1" to restore the Connected Standby feature, allowing quick power toggling on your Surface. Although you won't have access to all advanced settings, any changes made to a power plan will remain intact.

**Step 4: Using Command Prompt to Verify Power Plan Settings**

Once you've reactivated the "Connected Standby" feature, accessing most advanced power settings through the Control Panel's "Power Options" will no longer be possible. Here's how to ensure your advanced power settings are correctly configured:

1. Open Command Prompt or PowerShell.

2. Type "powercfg-list" and press Enter.

3. Copy the GUID (Globally Unique Identifier) of the power plan you created.

4. Type "powercfg -query GUID" (replace "GUID" with the actual GUID of your power plan) and press Enter.

   - Note: To copy text in Command Prompt, select the desired text and press Ctrl + C. To paste, right-click anywhere in the Command Prompt window.

5. Review the settings displayed. For example, you can set the maximum processor state to 100% when using AC power and 70% when using DC power.

By following these steps, you can ensure your power plan settings are accurately configured for optimal performance.

# Optimizing Cortana Settings

Optimizing Cortana Settings:

Cortana serves as a voice assistant for Windows 10, continuously running in the background to monitor your activities like speaking, writing, and typing. This data is sent to the Cortana server via your internet connection, syncing suggestions, reminders, alerts, and personalized preferences.

However, these activities can significantly drain your battery. To maximize battery life, it's advisable to minimize Cortana's tasks.

1. Click on the Cortana icon.

2. Select the gear icon.

3. Disable unnecessary options.

## Disabling Cortana On Windows 10 Anniversary Update:

Since the Windows 10 anniversary update, completely turning off Cortana via Settings is no longer possible. Instead, you'll need to utilize the Local Group Policy Editor to make changes to the Computer Configuration. Here's how:

1. Click "Start," type "gpedit.msc," and press "Enter."

2. Navigate to Computer Configuration > Administrative Templates > Windows Components > Search.

3. Double-click on "Allow Cortana to change the policy."

4. Choose "Turned Off."

5. Click "Apply" and then "OK."

## Turning Off Wi-Fi During Sleep:

When Connected Standby is enabled on a Surface device, pressing the power button puts the device into sleep mode rather than turning it off or hibernating, similar to phones and tablets. While in sleep mode, your Surface remains connected to Wi-Fi to receive emails and notifications.

However, disabling Wi-Fi during sleep conserves more battery life. Here's how:

1. Go to System > Power & Sleep.

2. Change the value in the "Network Connection" section to "Always."

## Adjusting Display Brightness:

Your computer screen's brightness can consume more power than other components. Microsoft recommends setting the brightness to 25% for optimal battery life on Surface devices. Additionally, disabling "Automatically adjust screen brightness" ensures your preferred brightness level is maintained.

To disable automatic brightness adjustment:

1. Go to Settings > System > Display.

2. Turn off "Change the brightness automatically when the light changes."

## Disabling Startup Programs:

Disabling unnecessary startup programs not only speeds up your computer's startup time but also reduces workload and conserves power.

To disable startup programs:

1. Open Task Manager.

2. Click on the Start-up tab.

3. Select the programs you wish to disable, then click "Disable."

## Browsing With Microsoft Edge:

Microsoft Edge, optimized for Microsoft Surface and Windows 10, offers efficiency advantages. According to discussions on Reddit, watching YouTube videos with Microsoft Edge utilizes the H.264 codec, which Intel Skylake processors decode more efficiently, reducing CPU power consumption.

Similarly, Microsoft Edge demonstrated superior battery life in tests streaming Netflix on identical Microsoft Surface Books.

## Google Chrome Optimization:

For Google Chrome users, addressing power consumption issues involves disabling the Flash Player plugin and installing H264IFY.

To disable the Flash Player plugin:

1. Open Chrome and navigate to the address bar.

2. Enter "chrome://plugins".

3. Click the "Disable" link under "Adobe Flash Player."

## Activating Battery Saver:

The Battery Saver feature is a recent addition to Windows 10, designed to prolong battery life by restricting background system activity and push notifications. To enable Battery Saver:

1. Navigate to Settings > System > Battery Saver > Battery Use > Change background app settings to manage background-running apps.

2. By activating Battery Saver, background-running apps will cease to operate, conserving battery life.

3. To activate Battery Saver, click on the battery icon in the taskbar and select Battery Saver.

On Surface PCs with the Power Slider feature enabled, simply slide the slider all the way to the left to activate Battery Saver.

## Disabling Bluetooth Radio:

Bluetooth plays a significant role in Surface Pro 4 and Surface Book functionalities, particularly when using the Surface Pen for tasks like activating OneNote, taking screenshots, or enabling Cortana.

However, if you don't require these features, you can conserve battery by turning off Bluetooth radio:

1. Open Settings > Devices > Bluetooth.

2. Deactivate the Bluetooth setting.

## Top 7 Apps for Microsoft Surface in 2024

An array of impressive apps tailored for Surface devices can be found on the Microsoft Store or other online platforms. To navigate through the multitude of options, here are 10 standout apps worth exploring:

**1. Best Microsoft Surface App for Crypto Trading: Crypto Chart**

**2. Best Surface App for Writing: Word**

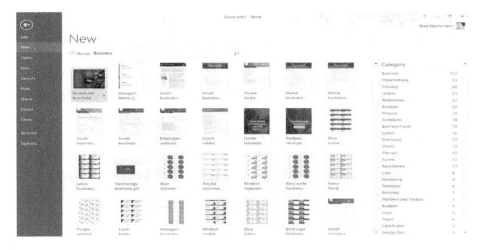

## 3. Best Windows Surface App for Stock Market Tracking: MSN Money

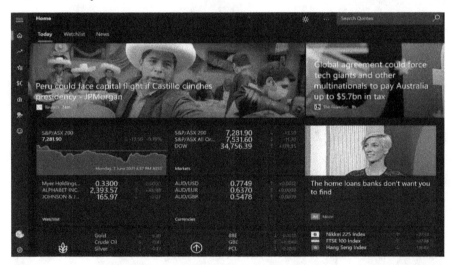

## 4. Best Surface App for Streaming on Twitch and YouTube: OBS Studio

## 5. Best Surface App for Audio Editing: Audacity

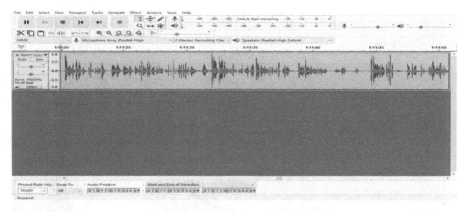

## 6. Best Windows Surface App for Exercising: Fitbit Coach

## 7. Best Streaming App for Surface: Netflix

These curated selections cater to a diverse range of interests and activities, ensuring an enriched experience for Surface users across various domains. Whether it's finance tracking, content creation, fitness, or entertainment, there's an app to suit every need and preference

# CHAPTER 10:

# TAKE SURFACE PRO 10 TO THE CLASS

### Taking Notes In Onenote:

Organize your notes in OneNote by creating a tab for each class and assigning a page to every assignment or date. Use your Surface Pen to jot down your thoughts and ideas.

### Finding Your Lost Surface Pen:

Retrieve your misplaced Surface Pen by following these steps:

1. Click "Start," then go to "Settings."

2. Navigate to "Update & Security," and select "Find my device" to track the last known usage location of your pen.

## Making Annotations On Web Pages:

Utilize Microsoft Edge to annotate web pages:

1. Click on "Settings and more" in Microsoft Edge.

2. Access "More tools," then "Add Notes." Here, you can write or draw on the page and share your annotations via email or social media.

## Leaving Your Notebook Behind:

Take advantage of OneNote's digital notebook capabilities, similar to using a physical notebook. Your notes are automatically saved to OneDrive, preventing any loss. Open OneNote, select "View," then enable "Rule Lines" to add grids or lines to your notes.

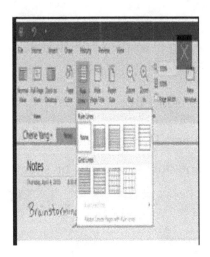

## Recording It:

Capture lectures by tapping "Insert," then selecting "Audio" to commence recording. Press the "Stop" button once you're finished. All notes made during the recording are saved in OneNote for future review. Use the "Replay" feature under "View" to jog your memory if needed.

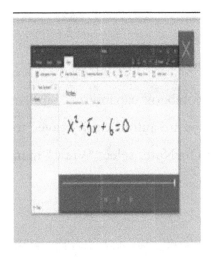

**Editing and Marking Up Files:**

Enhance PowerPoint, Excel, and Word files by editing and marking them up with your Surface Pen. Access the "Draw" menu for a quick and interactive way to express your thoughts.

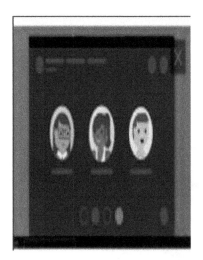

## Organizing With Microsoft Teams:

Utilize Microsoft Teams for streamlined organization:

Instead of relying on email, utilize Microsoft Teams to access files on OneDrive, conduct online meetings with Skype, and communicate with your group efficiently. It provides all the necessary tools for seamless collaboration on group projects.

# CHAPTER 11:

# CLEAN AND CARE FOR YOUR SURFACE PRO 10

## Keep Your Surface Clean

To keep your Surface clean, use a screen wipe or a soft, lint-free cloth with a bit of mild soap and water. You can choose how often you want to do this.

## Maximize Your Battery Life

Checking your battery level is really important, especially when you're in a place without power. Once a month, use your Surface until the battery is less than half full before charging it again.

## Clean Your Surface Touchscreen

After using your touchscreen, wipe it clean with a screen wipe or a soft, lint-free cloth. You can use it dry or slightly dampened with water or eyeglass cleaner, but avoid using chemical or glass cleaners.

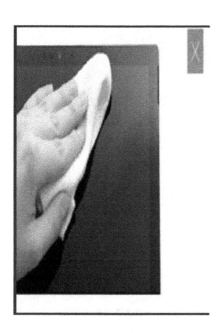

## Protect Your Surface Touchscreen

Dust, scratches, and sunlight can harm your touchscreen. Avoid leaving it in the sun for too long and make sure to cover it when not in use or during travels.

## Surface Type Cover and Touch Cover Care

Clean your cover with a soft cloth and mild soap and water (avoid getting liquids directly on it). If there's dirt or dust on the spine connections, use a damp cloth with a bit of rubbing alcohol.

## Alcantara® Material: General Care

To maintain the appearance of your Surface's Alcantara material, clean it with a soft white cloth dampened with water and mild soap. You can also use a screen cleaning wipe if necessary.

## Alcantara® Material: Removing Stains

If you spill something, clean it up quickly (ideally within 30 minutes). Use a white, soft cloth dampened with water and mild soap to remove the stain, then dry it with another clean, light-colored cloth.

# Surface Power Cord Care

Be careful not to pinch or bend the cord, and avoid wrapping it tightly around the power brick. When unplugging your Surface, pull on the connector instead of the cord.

# CHAPTER 12:

# SURFACE PRO 10 PEN: COLLABORATE, SAVE TIME AND EXPRESS YOURSELF

## Sign and Send Contracts

Instead of using a fax machine, save time by opening the contract file on your Surface. Use the Surface Pen to sign it (look for options like Ink, Add Notes, or Draw in any app). Once signed, send the contract via email to complete the process.

## Quickly Edit Website Updates

Before your website goes live, use your Surface Pen to indicate where changes are needed. Preview your site in Microsoft Edge, then select "Add notes." Tap on Share Web Note or Save Web Note, and mark the areas requiring changes.

## Collaborate on a PowerPoint Deck

Open a new PowerPoint file and click on the Draw tab. Use the Surface Pen to circle items, make annotations, and add notes. These comments can then be incorporated into the presentation.

## Bored? Draw with Surface Pen

Research suggests that doodling helps people remember information better. If you're in a dull meeting, grab your Surface Pen and start drawing to stay engaged.

## Give Feedback with Surface Pen

Easily edit and annotate files in Word, PowerPoint, or Excel using your Surface Pen. Look for the "Draw" menu, a simple and enjoyable way to share your thoughts.

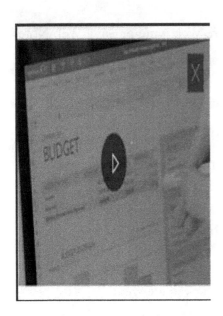

## Handwrite for Better Recall

In OneNote, jot down meeting notes using your Surface Pen (click on the Draw menu). Handwritten notes are proven to be easier to remember compared to typed ones.

## Color Stress Away with Surface Pen

Coloring has been shown to improve concentration and reduce stress. Explore coloring book apps available in the Microsoft Store to use with your Surface Pen.

## Writing as Meditative Practice

Spend a few minutes each day writing in a notebook or on OneNote. Express whatever comes to mind, even if it's "I don't know what to write." This practice can help you feel better and gain insights about yourself.

## More About the Surface Pen

Whether you're drawing, taking notes, or signing documents, the new and improved Surface Pen maximizes your productivity and creativity.

# CHAPTER 13:

# TRAVEL WITH YOUR SURFACE

## Plan Your Trip with Cortana

Simply tap on the Cortana icon and say, "Hello, Cortana. What's the quickest way to..." followed by your destination. Cortana will then find the fastest route from your current location.

## Travel Lighter

If you don't anticipate needing to type during your trip, leave your physical keyboard behind. Instead, add the touch keyboard to your taskbar for typing needs. Right-click on the taskbar and select "Show touch keyboard."

## Use a USB

Connect a USB adapter to the Surface Go's USB-C port, and then plug your USB device into the adapter for easy connectivity.

## Check Your Surface Accessory Power

Utilize the Surface app to check the power level of your Surface Pen or Mouse. Simply click on "Battery level" for more detailed information.

## Charge Everything Simultaneously

Take advantage of your Surface's power supply, many of which come with a built-in USB charging port. This allows you to charge both your Surface and your phone simultaneously.

## Navigate Offline

Planning a car trip? Download maps via Wi-Fi so you can navigate even without an internet connection. Go to Start, then click Settings > Apps > Offline Maps to get started.

## Keep The Kids Entertained

Research suggests that coloring and doodling can boost creativity and reduce stress. Keep your young travel companions entertained by giving them your Surface and Surface Pen to doodle and color.

## Have the Web Read Aloud to You

Microsoft Edge can read aloud e-books, PDFs, and web content. Simply tap or click anywhere on the page of an e-book, then select "Read aloud." For web content, click on "Settings and more," then choose "Read aloud."

## Switch to Airplane Mode

Prepare for takeoff by opening the action center with a tap of your touchpad using four fingers. Then, select "Flight mode." Tap again to switch it off when needed.

## Capture the Moment with Your Surface

Use the Surface's camera app to snap a photo. Select the picture from the camera roll and click "Share" to send it to an app or share it with others.

## Get Photos on Your Phone and Surface

Start the OneDrive app on your phone, sign in with your Microsoft account, and enable Camera Upload in the app settings. On your Surface, find the OneDrive icon on the right side of the taskbar (you may need to click the arrow to reveal hidden icons), then select "Open Folder" and click on the Camera Roll folder.

# CHAPTER 14:

# THE SURFACE PRO8CAMERA

# CAPTURE

## the whiteboard with your Surface

The Surface device comes equipped with a camera app that allows you to capture high-quality photos. By launching the camera app, you can utilize your device's camera to take pictures. Once you have taken a photo, it will be saved in the Camera Roll, which is a collection of all the photos and videos you have captured on your device. From there, you have the option to share the photo with others or send it to different applications for further editing or use.

## Adding Notes To A Photo With Your Surface:

If you want to add notes or thoughts to a picture, you can easily do so using your Surface device. Begin by opening the Camera app and capturing a photo. Afterward, navigate to the Camera Roll and select the desired image. To start adding notes, click on the "Edit & Create" option, which will provide you with various editing tools. From the available options, select "Draw." At this point, you can utilize your Surface Pen or any compatible stylus to write or draw directly on the photo. Once you are satisfied with the added notes, click "Save a copy" to preserve the edited version.

## Drawing On A Selfie Or Any Photo:

If you wish to draw on a selfie or any other photo, the Surface device offers a simple and intuitive process. To begin, open the Photos app, which provides access to all the images stored on your device. Locate the particular photo you want to edit and tap on it. This action will present you with editing options, including "Edit & Create." By selecting this option, you will be able to access various editing tools. Choose the "Draw" option, which will enable you to select different drawing tools such as brushes, pens, or pencils. With these tools, you can freely draw on the photo using your finger, mouse, or a paired pen. This feature allows for a creative and personalized touch to your pictures.

# CHAPTER 15:

# SAVE MORE TIME WITH SURFACE PRO 10

## Making Your Battery Last Longer:

To optimize the battery life of your device, you can activate the power saver feature. This can be done by accessing the action center, which is located on the taskbar. Simply click on the action center icon and then choose the Battery Saver option. Enabling this feature helps conserve power by adjusting certain settings to minimize energy consumption.

## Capturing a Whiteboard with Your Surface Pro 10:

If you're using a Surface Pro 10 and want to capture the contents of a whiteboard, you can utilize the Camera app. By opening the Camera app on your device, you can take a picture of the whiteboard. Once you have captured the image, you can access it in the Camera Roll. To share the photo with others or send it to another app, click on the picture in the Camera Roll and select the Share option. This allows you to easily distribute or utilize the image as needed.

## Translating Text on the Fly:

If you need to translate text while working in Word, you can take advantage of the translation feature. Simply select the text you want to translate, right-click on it, and choose the "Translate" option. This will provide you with the ability to select the desired language for the translation. Once you have chosen the language, click on Insert to add the translated text to your document. This feature helps you easily understand and work with text in different languages.

# Filling Forms with a Click:

To streamline the process of filling out web forms, Microsoft Edge offers an autofill feature. When you encounter a web form, you can let Microsoft Edge automatically fill in the required information for you. To manage your autofill settings or make changes, click on "Settings and more" (represented by three dots) in the browser's toolbar. Then, navigate to Settings, select Passwords & auto-fill, and click on Manage forms. From there, you can modify or add information as needed.

# Efficient Cell Filling in Excel:

Excel provides a handy feature that automatically fills in cells based on the information you input. Once you start typing in a cell, Excel analyzes the pattern and fills in the adjacent cells accordingly. If Excel suggests the correct information, you can simply press the Enter key to accept the suggestion. This feature saves time and effort when working with large sets of data in Excel.

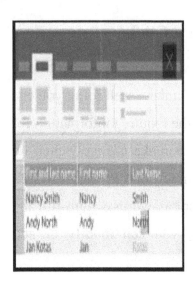

## Giving Feedback with Surface Pen:

If you have a Surface Pen, you can utilize it to mark up and make changes to PowerPoint, Excel, and Word files. Look for the "Draw" menu within these applications. It provides a variety of tools and options that allow you to annotate, highlight, and provide feedback directly on the files. This feature enhances collaboration and facilitates clear communication when reviewing and editing documents.

## Jumping Between Apps:

To quickly switch between different apps on your device, you can use a multitouch gesture. Place three fingers on your touchpad and swipe right or left to navigate between open applications. This gesture allows for efficient multitasking and smooth transitions between various tasks or projects.

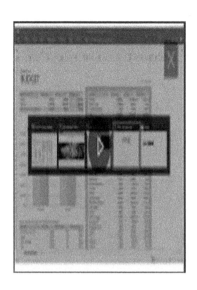

## Save Time While You Type

To enhance your typing experience, you can enable text suggestions, which provide predictive text options as you type. By clicking on Start, then going to Settings, followed by Devices, Typing, Hardware Keyboard, and finally, Show text suggestions as I type, you can activate this feature. As you type, you'll see suggested words or phrases that you can select with a single click, saving you time and reducing typing efforts.

## Locking Your PC in a Second:

To ensure the security of your PC when you step away, you can quickly lock it by pressing the Windows key and the letter L simultaneously. This action instantly locks your PC, requiring a password or other authentication method to regain access. It's a simple and effective way to protect your privacy and prevent unauthorized access to your device.

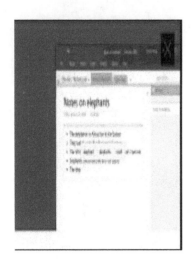

# CHAPTER 16:

# HOW TO ACCESS THE SURFACE'S BATTERY REPORT

Battery Report is a useful tool that provides insights into your Surface device's battery usage and behavior. By utilizing this feature, you can gather detailed information about your battery and its changes over time. Continue reading to explore more about the report, including how to generate and access it.

Windows includes a powerful power management tool that offers valuable knowledge about your battery's functionality and its evolution. This tool is called "Battery Report" and offers a comprehensive overview of your battery's performance. The report consists of the following sections:

## Basic Computer And OS Information

Information about the batteries currently installed in your device, including details about each battery.

The power states that have been utilized within the past three days.

The amount of battery usage and depletion experienced in the last three days.

A usage history that records how the system has been utilized on both AC power and the battery.

The historical data of the system's batteries, including their charging capacity.

Estimates of battery life are derived from analyzing the rate at which the battery is consumed.

## How to Access the Battery Report

To access the battery report, you need to create a report that displays your current battery information and your past battery usage. Follow these steps:

1. Right-click on the "Start" button located on your screen.
2. From the options that appear, select "Command Prompt."
3. In the Command Prompt window, type "powercfg /batteryreport" and then press the Enter key on your keyboard. This action generates a report that provides insights into how long your battery is expected to last. The report will be saved in the current location as a file named "battery-report.html." It contains comprehensive information about the battery of your current device. For more accurate information, it is recommended to perform a full recharge cycle multiple times. This method is applicable to all Surface devices, including those running Windows RT, Windows 8.1, and Windows 10.

## Best Accessories for Microsoft Surface

By equipping your Surface device with the appropriate accessories, you can significantly enhance its productivity. Below, we have listed some of the top accessories that we recommend for Surface devices.

These accessories are essential additions that can improve your experience with Microsoft Surface devices. With the inclusion of a Surface Pen, Surface Dock, Surface Precision Mouse, and a microSD card, your Surface device will operate more efficiently, provide increased storage capacity, and enable you to accomplish tasks more effectively.

# CHAPTER 17:

# HOW TO TAKE A SCREENSHOT ON YOUR SURFACE 10

To capture a screenshot of your entire screen on a Surface device, simultaneously press and hold the volume up button and the power button. Once captured, you can easily paste the screenshot into various applications, emails, or documents. The screenshot will also be automatically saved in a dedicated folder named "Screenshots."

## How To Screenshot On Surface Pro 10: The 6 Fast And Easy Ways

In this guide, we will explain six different ways to capture screenshots on a 2024 Surface Pro 10. We will cover using the hardware buttons, keyboard shortcuts, Surface Pen, and the built-in Windows tools to help you easily capture and save screenshots.

The Surface Pro 10, equipped with the latest 8th Gen Intel® processors, represents a significant advancement in productivity tools for 2024. With an increased number of CPU cores, from 2 to 4, it offers improved performance. This device is particularly well-suited for digital artists, students, and professionals who require a powerful yet portable device. If you are transitioning from another laptop, you may find it initially challenging to capture screenshots on the Surface Pro 10, especially when it is in tablet mode.

The 2024 Surface Pro 10 running Windows 10 offers a wide range of functionalities beyond just capturing screenshots. Discover the most suitable method for your needs by continuing to read below.

Method 1: Capturing a Screenshot on Surface Pro 10 using Physical Buttons

Method 2: Taking a Screenshot on Surface Pro 10 with the Surface Type Cover

Method 3: Using the Surface Pen to Capture a Picture on Surface Pro 10

Method 4: Utilizing the Windows Snipping Tool to Take Screenshots on Surface Pro 10

Method 5: Taking a Screenshot of your Surface Pro 10 with the Snip & Sketch Tool

Method 6: Capturing Screenshots on Surface Pro 10 using Shortcut Keys

## Method 1: Capturing A Screenshot On Surface Pro 10 Using Hardware Buttons

This method is particularly useful if you prefer using your Surface device as a tablet, without the attached type cover. Follow these simple steps to take a screenshot using the hardware buttons on your Surface Pro 10:

1. Press and hold down the power button located on your device.

2. While continuing to hold down the power button, press the Volume Up button on the side of the device once, and then release it.
3. You will notice a momentary dimming and brightening of the screen, indicating that a screenshot has been successfully captured.

Note: All the screenshots taken using this method will be automatically saved in a designated folder called "Screenshots" within the Pictures library.

**Method 2: Capturing A Screenshot On Surface Pro 10 With Surface Type Cover**

If you have a Surface Type Cover attached to your device, you can utilize the PrtSn (Print Screen) key on the keyboard to capture screenshots, just as you have done before. Here are two options to choose from:

*Option 1:* Capturing a Screenshot of the Entire Screen and Saving it to the Windows Clipboard

1. Press the PrtSn key on your keyboard to capture a screenshot of the entire screen.
2. Open a program of your choice, such as Paint or Word, and paste the screenshot from the Windows Clipboard into the program.

*Option 2:* Capturing a Screenshot of the Active Window and Saving it to the Windows Clipboard

1. To capture a screenshot of the active window, simultaneously press the Alt key and the PrtSn key on your keyboard.
2. Open a program of your choice, such as Paint or Word, and paste the screenshot from the Windows Clipboard into the program.

**Method 3: Capturing A Screenshot On Surface Pro 10 With Surface Pen**

The Surface Pen has been designed to offer enhanced functionality with Windows 10. One of the new features introduced in the Windows 10 anniversary update is Screen Sketch. This feature allows you to capture the device's screen and access tools for drawing, cropping, and more.

With this functionality, you can use the Surface Pen to capture a screenshot. Follow these steps to utilize the Screen Sketch feature:

- Double-click the eraser button located on the top of the Surface Pen.
- On the screen, you will see various tools, including the "Save as" button located in the top right corner. Click on this button to access options for editing, cropping, and saving the screenshot.

## Method 4: Using The Windows Snipping Tool To Capture A Screenshot On Surface Pro 10

Windows provides a built-in program called the "Snipping Tool" that offers more controls and features for capturing screenshots compared to the previous methods. To begin using it, follow these steps:

1. Open the Start menu and type "Snipping Tool" directly into the Cortana search box.

Alternatively, you can navigate to the Windows Accessories folder within the Start menu to locate the Snipping Tool.

2. Once the Snipping Tool is open, you can choose from four different screenshot modes:

- Capture the entire screen.
- Capture a specific program window.
- Capture a rectangular area of any size on the screen.
- Capture a custom shape drawn by hand.

3. After selecting the desired screen area to capture, it will appear in a new window. Before saving the screenshot, you have the option to draw or highlight specific parts of the image.

4. Finally, save the screenshot in the format of your choice, such as JPEG, PNG, GIF, or HTML, depending on your preference and requirements.

**Method 5: Using The Snip & Sketch Tool To Capture A Screenshot On Surface Pro 10**

In recent updates of Windows 10, Microsoft introduced a modern tool called Snip & Sketch. This tool allows you to easily annotate screenshots, photos, and other images using your pen, touch, or mouse. You can then save, paste, or share these annotated images with other applications. To capture a screenshot using this tool, follow these steps:

1. Open the Start menu or Cortana text box and type "Snip & Sketch." Alternatively, you can locate the Snip & Sketch app in the Start menu and open it from there.
2. Once the Snip & Sketch tool is open, click on the "New" button, and then select "Snip Now."
3. Choose the specific area of your Surface Pro 10's screen that you want to capture.
4. The captured image will appear in a new Snip & Sketch window. At this point, you can write on the screenshot, draw on it, or highlight any elements you desire.
5. To save the screenshot as a file, click the "Save" button. Alternatively, you can click the "Copy" icon to copy the screenshot to the Windows clipboard, allowing you to paste it into other applications or documents.

## Method 6: Capturing A Screenshot On Surface Pro 10 Using Shortcut Keys

You can save time by using shortcut keys in Windows 10 to quickly access the Snip & Sketch tool on your Surface Pro 10. To utilize this method, follow these steps:

1. Press and hold the Windows key and Shift key simultaneously, and then press the S key.

This keyboard combination will instantly launch the Snip & Sketch tool in screen clipping mode, allowing you to immediately select and capture any desired part of the screen.

2. Once the Snip & Sketch tool is activated, you can enhance the screenshot by adding notes, drawing on it, or making it more prominent using the available tools.
3. To save the screenshot as a file, simply click the "Save" button. Alternatively, you can click the "Copy" button to copy the screenshot to the Windows clipboard, enabling you to paste it into other applications or documents.

These are the six methods available for capturing screenshots on your Surface Pro 10, providing you with a range of options to suit your preferences.

# CHAPTER 18:

# HOW TO USE YOUR SURFACE PRO 10 AS A PORTABLE DISPLAY

Are you using a Surface Pro 3? If so, you'll be pleased to know that it supports mouse, keyboard, touch, and pen input. This means you can utilize your Surface device as a convenient and portable wireless display or as a second screen. Having multiple monitors can significantly enhance your productivity by allowing you to multitask effectively.

In my own office setup, I have three monitors: the primary display on my Surface Book, a spacious 29-inch ultra-wide monitor, and two 21.5-inch monitors on either side. With this arrangement, I can easily view up to six websites simultaneously, conduct research, write articles, and perform various tasks concurrently. Even when I'm away from my office, I have a portable setup that enables me to work with multiple monitors.

Although I don't possess a dedicated portable monitor, I make use of my Surface Pro as a portable wireless display. It serves me well for web browsing and most other tasks, providing a satisfactory experience on the go.

# Configuring a Surface Pro8as a Portable Monitor

You can configure your Surface Pro 10 as a wireless display by following these steps:

1. Open the Settings on your device.
2. Select the "System" option.
3. Click on "Project to this PC."
4. In the first option, choose either "Available everywhere" or "Available everywhere on secure networks."
5. In the second option, select either "Only the first time" or "Every time a connection is requested." If you prefer not to confirm each connection, choose "First time only."
6. For added security, enable the "Required PIN for pairing" option.
7. If you want to use your Surface Pro as a portable display, ensure that the "This PC can only be found for projection when it is plugged in" setting is turned off.
8. Lastly, when projecting from another computer to your Surface Pro, you will be prompted to confirm by selecting "Yes."

## Projecting The Surface Pro8to A Wireless Display

Setting up Surface PC (Surface 3) for Projection from Main PC (Surface Book)

Once you have configured your Surface PC (Surface 3) to accept projection from your main PC (Surface Book), follow these steps:

1. Open the Action Centre on your Surface PC.

2. Click on the "Connect" button.

3. Choose the desired remote wireless display device by selecting its name. Depending on your specific setup, you may need to use another compatible device to test the connection. If the link does not work, you will need to retry the process.

4. Once connected, if you wish to use the mouse, keyboard, touch, and pen input from the remote computer (Surface 3) on your main PC (Surface Book), disable the "Allow input from a keyboard or mouse connected to this display" option.

5. You can also adjust the projection mode, similar to changing settings for a physical monitor, by clicking on "Change projection mode" or pressing the Win+P keys on your keyboard.

6. When you have finished your work, click on "Disconnect" to terminate the connection.

# CHAPTER 19:

# TUNE IN WITH YOUR SURFACE HEADPHONES

Using Surface Headphones With Your Computer

To connect your Surface Headphones to your computer, follow these steps:

1. Press and hold the power button on your Surface Headphones for 5 seconds.
2. When you hear the prompt, "You're ready to pair," release the power button.
3. Once your computer detects the headphones, a notification will appear.
4. Click on "Connect" to establish the connection.

## Adjusting The Volume

To increase the volume on your Surface headphones, rotate the right dial forward. To decrease the volume, rotate the right dial in the opposite direction.

## Blocking External Sounds

To minimize distractions from your surroundings, rotate the left dial forward while wearing your Surface headphones. This action will activate noise cancellation, reducing external noise.

## Controlling Your Music With Taps

To manage your music playback, use the touchpad on either ear of the headphones. A single tap will play or pause the music. Double-tapping will skip to the next song, while triple-tapping will go back to the previous song.

## Muting The Microphone

To mute the microphone on your Surface headphones, press the "Mute" button located on the right ear. This action will disable the microphone. When you are ready to speak again, tap the same button to unmute the microphone.

# CHAPTER 20:

# HOW TO UNLOCK POWER PLANS ON SURFACE DEVICES

Understanding Connected Standby and Modern Standby on Microsoft Surface Devices

In this guide, you will discover the concepts of Connected Standby and Modern Standby, as well as how to access all power plans and advanced settings on Microsoft Surface devices. Microsoft has introduced a feature called "Connected Standby" in Windows 8, which has been further enhanced and integrated into Windows 10 as Modern Standby. Modern Standby allows your system to operate in either connected standby or disconnected standby mode, depending on the hardware and software configuration.

## What is Modern Standby?

With Modern Standby, your PC can be powered on or off as swiftly as your smartphone. Similar to a phone, it remains up-to-date when connected to Wi-Fi or a reliable network, even during standby mode.

There are three key reasons to consider using Modern Standby:

1. Instant power control: Like smartphones, Windows PCs and tablets equipped with Modern Standby can be powered on and off instantly.

2. Background activity during "off" state: This feature enables your PC or tablet to perform tasks from Windows Store apps in the background even when the system appears to be "off."

3. Improved wake-up functionality: In contrast to previous models, a hardware interrupt alone can now wake up a system from standby mode.

By familiarizing yourself with Connected Standby and Modern Standby, you can take full advantage of the power management capabilities on your Microsoft Surface device, optimizing its performance and energy efficiency.

## Power Plans On Surface Devices

When you first receive your Microsoft Surface device, it comes with a pre-configured power plan called "Balanced." Additionally, there are a few advanced settings available, as listed below:

Due to the default activation of Connected Standby on all Surface devices, the power settings in Advanced Settings are limited. Surface devices intelligently manage these advanced settings and keep them hidden.

To unlock and utilize all available power plans and advanced settings, you need to disable Connected Standby through the Registry Editor. Follow these steps:

1. Press the Windows key + R on your keyboard.
2. Type "regedit" to launch the Registry Editor.

3.  Navigate                                                    to
    "HKEY_LOCAL_MACHINE\SYSTEM\CurrentControlSet\C
    ontrol\Power."
4.  Double-click on "CsEnabled."
5.  Change the value data from "1" to "0."
6.  Click "OK."
7.  Restart your computer for the changes to take effect.

After restarting your computer, you can now select from various power plans such as Power Saver, Balanced, and High Performance. Disabling Connected Standby also enables you to access advanced settings for each power plan you choose.

8.  When you have finished making changes, click "OK" to save them.

Please note that disabling Connected Standby will remove the ability of the Surface Pen to instantly turn the Surface on or off and open OneNote while the device is in standby mode. Instead, pressing the power button will put your Surface to sleep.

Once you have customized your power plans and settings, you can re-enable Connected Standby to regain those features. Even after enabling Connected Standby, all your plans and settings will remain intact.

To turn Connected Standby back on, return to the Registry Editor, change the value data of "CsEnabled" back to 1, and restart your computer. This will restore the modern standby features while preserving your plans and settings.

By following these steps, you can effectively configure power plans and advanced settings on your Surface device, tailoring them to your specific preferences and optimizing power management.

# CHAPTER 21:

# HOW TO NAVIGATE WITH THE USE OF YOUR SURFACE TOUCHSCREEN

1. Making Quick Changes: Easily swipe from the right side of your screen to access a menu for making swift adjustments.

2. Action Center for Notifications and Settings: The action center allows you to view notifications and modify settings such as network connections, airplane mode, and Bluetooth with just a few taps.

3. Swipe Across the Right Side of the Screen: Move your finger horizontally along the right side of your touch screen to perform this action.

## Switching Between Apps With A Swipe

1. Swipe from the left side of your Surface's touchscreen to access a menu showing all your apps. It enables you to swiftly switch between them and view your entire collection.

2. Closing Apps: In the Task menu, you also have the option to close an app.

3. Adjusting App Size and Viewing Title Bar: Drag your finger downward from the top of the screen to change the app's size or reveal the title bar.

4. Resizing Apps: By swiping downward from the top of the Surface touchscreen, you can reduce the size of a large app.

5. Viewing Title Bar in Full-Screen Mode: If an app, like OneNote, is in full-screen mode, you can swipe down to display the title bar.

6. Accessing the Taskbar: Drag your finger upward from the bottom of the screen to access the taskbar.

7. Taskbar Access with Full-Screen App: When an app occupies the entire screen, you can swipe up from the bottom of the touch screen to reach the taskbar.

8. Hiding Apps: Tap anywhere on the touch screen to hide the app you're currently using.

9. Selecting and Opening Items: Use your finger to tap on items or apps on your Surface's touch screen, similar to how you interact with your phone.

10. Exploring More by Touch and Hold: Touch and hold an item to discover additional information.

11. Interacting with Hold: Place your finger on the item and hold it for a second to access more details or open a menu, similar to using the right-click function on a mouse.

## Zooming In And Out With Pinch Or Stretch Gestures

You can easily zoom in and out on your device by using a pinch or stretch gesture on its touch screen.

1. Zooming In: Place two fingers on the screen and move them away from each other to zoom in.

2. Zooming Out: Bring your two fingers closer together on the screen to zoom out.

# Dragging Up And Down To Scroll

You can scroll vertically or horizontally on your device's touch screen, just like you would on a phone. Simply move your finger up and down on the screen to scroll in the desired direction. You can also use your finger to select items.

1. Moving Items: Press and hold an item with your finger and then move it to a different location on the screen.
2. Dragging to Select: By dragging your finger across the surface of the touch screen, you can quickly select multiple items.
3. Quick Item Selection: Use a swift flick of your finger to select an item with ease.

# CHAPTER 22:

# DOWNLOADING AND INSTALLING THE LATEST SURFACE PRO 10 DRIVERS AND FIRMWARE UPDATES

If necessary, you can now download the firmware update and all the drivers for the 2024 Surface Pro 10. This is particularly useful for troubleshooting driver issues or performing a clean installation. In business environments where multiple 2024 Surface Pro 10 devices need to be set up, it becomes even more important.

Microsoft frequently updates these downloads, so it's advisable to regularly check the download page whenever the need arises. If you have internet connectivity, it is recommended to utilize Windows Update for acquiring the latest drivers and firmware updates.

## Current Drivers And Firmware And Cumulative For Surface Pro 10

The Drivers and Firmware package contains all ·the necessary drivers and system updates for the Surface Pro 10. These drivers are compatible with Windows 10, including Enterprise versions. The firmware and drivers required by Surface devices are included in the driver MSI files, which are utilized for Windows custom images.

### Obtaining The Latest Drivers And Firmware

To acquire the drivers and firmware for the Surface Pro 10, follow these steps:

1. Visit the download page dedicated to Surface Pro 10 drivers and firmware.
2. Click on the "Download" button.

Note:

The update files can be named differently, taking into account the following parameters: "Surface Model," "Windows Version," "Minimum Build Requirement," "Driver Release Number," "Upload Number," and the file extension.

3. Select all the files you need to download, and then proceed by clicking "Next."

4. Finally, click on "Save" to complete the download process.

## Manual Installation Of Updates

Once you have completed the download process, you can proceed with the installation. Follow these steps:

1.  Double-click on the downloaded .msi file.
2.  The installation screen will appear. Tap "Next" to proceed.

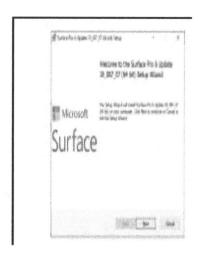

3.  Agree to the terms and conditions, then click "Next" to continue.

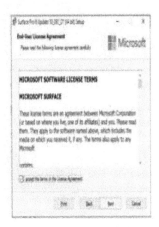

4. Choose the desired installation location and click "Next" to proceed.

5. Press the "Install" button to initiate the setup process.

6. The installation may take approximately 10 minutes to complete. Once finished, click "Finish" to complete the setup.

7. To finalize the system update, it is necessary to turn off and then turn on the Surface Pro 10. Tap "Yes" to proceed with the restart.

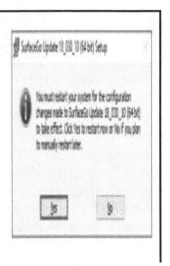

**Comprehensive Testing Of Surface Pro 10 Firmware And Drivers**

If you're unsure about the version of your device, you can easily determine it by checking your current installation.

1. Go to Settings, then select Apps, followed by Apps & Features.
2. Look for "SurfacePro6 Update xx xxx xx (64 bit)" in the list of installed applications.

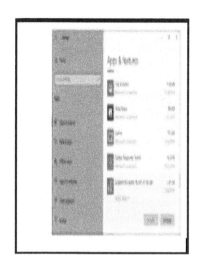

# CHAPTER 24:

# DO MORE WITH YOUR SURFACE PRO 10 PEN

The Surface Pen allows you to write and draw on your Surface device, providing a paper-like experience. It can also function as a mouse, enabling interaction with the touch screen. When not in use, you can conveniently attach the pen to the left side of your screen using the built-in magnet.

Before using your Surface Pen, especially for the first time, you need to pair it with your device. Follow these steps:

1. On your PC, click the "Start" button.
2. Tap or click on "Settings."
3. Select "Devices."
4. Choose "Bluetooth and other devices."
5. Ensure that "Bluetooth" is turned on.
6. Tap "Add other devices or Bluetooth."
7. Press the "Bluetooth" button on the pen.

8. Press and hold the top button of the pen for five to seven seconds, then release it. The light on the flat side of the pen will turn green.

9. A list of devices will appear, and you should select "Surface Pen" from the list.

10. Follow the on-screen instructions that appear.

11. Select "Done."

## Surface Dial

The Surface Dial enhances the usability of your apps and Surface device. To get started, you need to connect your Surface Dial by following these steps:

1. On your PC, click the "Start" button.

2. Tap or click on "Settings."

3. Select "Devices."

4. Choose "Bluetooth and other devices."

5. Ensure that "Bluetooth" is turned on.

6. Tap "Add other devices or Bluetooth."

7. Select "Bluetooth" in step 7.

8. Pull down on the bottom of your Surface Dial to open the battery compartment. Make sure there are two AAA batteries inside.

9. Remove the battery tab from the bottom of the Surface Dial.

10. Press and hold the button near the batteries for five to seven seconds, then release it. The Bluetooth light will flash upon release.

11. A list of devices will appear, and you should select the Surface Dial from that list.

12. Follow the on-screen instructions that appear.

13. Select "Done."

# Get The Most Out Of Your Surface Pen

## Using Surface Dial And Paint 3D

## Take Advantage Of Surface Dial To Enhance Your Paint 3D Experience:

Choose Colors with Surface Dial

After launching Paint 3D, long-press Surface Dial to access the color palette. Rotate the Surface Dial to select a different color, and then tap it to confirm your choice.

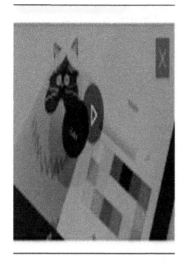

## Rotate Objects With Surface Dial

In Paint 3D, unleash your creativity by drawing any object using the 3D tools or selecting from Remix 3D. Click on Art Tools, choose a brush, and start painting. While adding colors to the object, turn the Surface Dial to rotate it.

**Experiment Freely And Easily Revert**

Made a mistake? Open Paint 3D, hold down the Surface Dial button for a while, and select History. Use the Surface Dial to navigate through your changes and review your progress.

## Erase With The Surface Pen

Similar to using a pencil, you can erase using the top button on the Surface Pen. To do this, utilize the Windows Ink Workspace.

## Select Items With The Surface Pen

To make a selection, move the Surface Pen around the screen while holding down the barrel button.

## Scroll With Your Surface Pen

Say goodbye to searching for scroll bars. To scroll through a webpage, simply move the Surface Pen up or down on the screen, just like you would with your finger. Let us know if you write with your right or left hand!

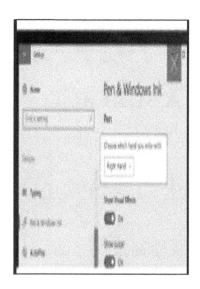

## Optimize Handwriting Recognition

Improve the Surface Pen's ability to read your handwriting by specifying your writing hand. Click "Start," then "Settings," followed by "Devices," and select "Pen & Windows Ink."

## Customize App Shortcuts

Add a shortcut button to the top of your Surface Pen for quick access to your preferred app. Click "Start," then "Settings," followed by "Devices," and select "Pen & Windows Ink." Choose the desired app from the list of shortcuts.

# CHAPTER 25:

# HOW TO CONNECT A SURFACE MOBILE MOUSE TO YOUR COMPUTER

If you're experiencing difficulties in getting your Surface Mobile Mouse to work with your Surface device or computer, the following instructions will provide you with the necessary information.

The Surface Mobile Mouse is one of Microsoft's recent additions to their lineup of affordable mouse options. It was introduced on July 10, 2018, alongside the Microsoft Surface Go. Designed to be lightweight and portable, it is available in three stylish colors: platinum, cobalt blue, and burgundy. Compatible with various laptops, including the Microsoft Surface Go, Laptop, Pro, Book, and others, it offers versatility.

This mouse utilizes Bluetooth low energy version 4.0 or 4.1, allowing you to connect it to both desktops and laptops. However, it's important to ensure that your computer is equipped with a Bluetooth adapter or module. Continue reading to learn how to set up your Surface Mobile Mouse for use with your computer.

Note: All Surface devices, including Surface RT, are equipped with a Bluetooth module that supports Bluetooth low energy version 4.0. This enables you to connect the Surface Mobile Mouse to any other Surface device.

## Connecting Surface Mobile Mouse Using The Swift Pair Feature

Windows 10 and other new Bluetooth devices introduce a convenient feature called "Bluetooth Swift Pair." This feature allows users to quickly connect to supported Bluetooth devices in close proximity through a simple alert. The Surface Mobile Mouse is compatible with this feature, and it's essential to understand how to use it effectively. Follow these steps:

### Step 1: Activating Pairing Mode

- Check if your computer supports Windows 10 and Bluetooth LE 4.0.

- Flip the switch located below the Surface Mobile Mouse to turn on Bluetooth. The LED light will illuminate, indicating it's powered on.

---

- Press and hold the Bluetooth button on the mouse for approximately 3–5 seconds. The LED light on the mouse's underside will blink until it successfully pairs.

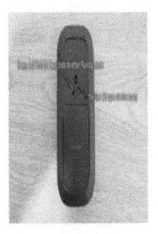

**Step 2: Allowing Computer Connection Request**

1. Place the Surface Mobile Mouse near your computer.

2. Within a few seconds, Windows will display a message.

3. Tap "Connect" to initiate the pairing process.

4. A notification will confirm the successful connection of your Surface Mobile Mouse.

# How To Set Up The Surface Mobile Mouse To Work With Bluetooth

If the initial method doesn't succeed, you can attempt to connect the Surface Mobile Mouse using the traditional pairing approach. This option can be found in the Bluetooth settings. Follow the instructions below as a reference:

1. Refer to the previous steps to activate Pairing Mode on the Surface Mobile Mouse.
2. Click or select the Action Center icon.
3. Long-press the Bluetooth button or right-click it on your PC.
4. Choose "Go to Settings."

5. Tap "Add Bluetooth or other device."

6. Select Bluetooth.

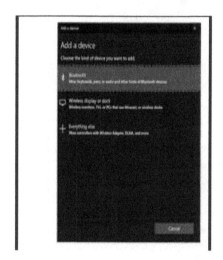

7. Choose the "Surface Mobile Mouse" option.

8.  Tap "Done."

Your Windows 10 computer is now configured to utilize the Surface Mobile Mouse.

# Alternatively, How To: Connect Surface Precision Mouse Via Bluetooth

The Microsoft Surface Precision Mouse allows you to connect it wirelessly to your computer and even switch between up to three computers seamlessly. Follow these steps to connect your Microsoft Surface Mouse to your computer:

1.  Ensure that your computer supports Bluetooth LE 4.0, or enable Bluetooth if needed.
2.  Press the power button located at the bottom of your Surface Precision Mouse to turn it on.

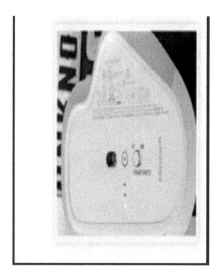

3.  Tap the Bluetooth button to select the desired connection from the three available options.
4.  Press and hold the Bluetooth button for 3–5 seconds. The light corresponding to the selected connection slot will start blinking, indicating pairing mode.

5. Click the Action Center icon, press and hold the Bluetooth key, or right-click it and select "Go to settings."

6. Click on "Add Bluetooth or other device."

7. Select Bluetooth.

8. Choose the "BTLE precision mouse" option.

9. Follow the on-screen instructions to complete the setup.

Your Windows 10 computer is now successfully connected to the Surface Precision Mouse, and you can start using it.

## Connecting Your Surface Precision Mouse Using A Micro USB Cable

1. Here's how to connect your Surface Precision Mouse to your computer using the appropriate Micro USB cable.

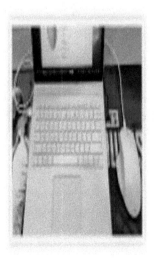

2. After installing the required software, the Surface Precision Mouse will appear in the software interface.

---

Now you have the knowledge to connect the Surface Precision Mouse to other Surface devices and Windows 10. However, the Micro USB connection method offers the advantage of compatibility with any computer, regardless of Bluetooth support.

## Replacing The Batteries Of The Surface Arc Mouse

If you're unsure about setting up the Surface Arc Mouse or replacing its batteries, this page provides straightforward instructions to guide you through the process.

The Surface Arc Mouse is Microsoft's most portable mouse to date. It was released on May 2, 2017, alongside the Microsoft Surface Laptop. This sleek and lightweight mouse is available in three colors: light gray, burgundy, and cobalt blue.

The Surface Arc Mouse is powered by two AAA batteries, which can be easily replaced. With regular usage, these batteries can last up to 9 months. Today, we'll demonstrate how to insert or change the batteries in the Surface Arc Mouse.

Replacing the batteries in the Surface Arc Mouse is a simple process. Follow these steps:

1.  Press the eject button located on the bottom of the mouse and remove the battery cover.

2.  Use your fingernail or a flat screwdriver to push and release the old batteries.

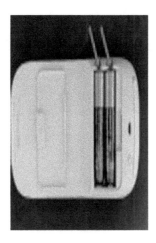

3. Insert the new batteries following the orientation indicated by the battery slot markings.

4. Replace the battery cover, ensuring it is securely in place. To verify proper battery installation, turn on the mouse and check if the laser pointer is functioning.

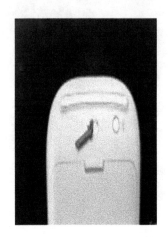

# CHAPTER 26:

# 10 MICROSOFT SURFACE PRO 10 TIPS & TRICKS

Discover ten essential tips and tricks to maximize your Surface experience.

When you find yourself disoriented, simply swipe in from the left side of the screen.

**When You Remove An App, The Start Screen Automatically Fills The Empty Space.**

However, what were you doing before you clicked on the link and got distracted? To find out, simply swipe your finger in from the left edge of the screen. By dragging your original app back onto the screen, you can easily return to where you were before the interruption.

**Type Right On The Start Screen To Look For Things.**

If you have connected a keyboard to your Surface, you'll enjoy a special advantage. You can directly type the name of what you're looking for on the Start screen.

Windows will display the Charms bar, enter your search query into the search field, and begin showing you relevant matches.

To perform the same action, click on the search icon located in the upper-right corner of the Start screen. This will bring up the search field within the search pane. Simply tap on the search field to display the on-screen keyboard. From there, you can type in the desired words you wish to find.

**Choose Things On The Screen Within Apps.**

To pick up objects, simply move your finger in the opposite direction of their scrolling motion.

In the Mail app, you can usually navigate through your emails by dragging your finger up and down the list. To choose a single email, swipe your finger left or right over it. This method of sliding in the opposite direction can also be applied to other scenarios where choosing between multiple options may appear challenging.

**Capturing Screenshots**

To take a screenshot on your Surface device, follow these steps:

1. Press and hold the Windows key located below the screen.

2. While holding the Windows key, press the Volume Down button.

3. The screen will briefly go dark, indicating that a screenshot has been taken.

4. You can find the captured screenshot in the Screenshots folder within your Pictures collection.

When encountering an error message, it can be highly beneficial to take a screenshot. This allows you to share the screenshot with a technical support person who can assist in identifying and resolving the issue at hand.

**Prevent Screen Rotation**

In certain situations, such as reading a book or browsing the internet, you may prefer to keep your screen orientation fixed.

To disable screen rotation, follow these steps:

1. Open the Charms bar and click on Settings.

2. Once the Settings pane appears, locate and tap on the Screen icon situated in the bottom right corner.

3. Look for the Rotation Lock icon positioned at the top of the brightness bar.

4. Touch the Rotation Lock icon to toggle the autorotation feature on or off, according to your preference.

**Modify The Functionality Of Your App.**

Each app has a Settings section in the Charms bar that allows you to customize its behavior. If there's something you don't like about an app, try adjusting it. To access the charms bar, swipe your finger from the right side of the screen and tap on the Settings icon. If a particular app allows for settings modification, you can make the changes in the Settings pane.

**Create A Drive For Recovery.**

Creating a recovery drive is a straightforward process. If you have a flash drive available, you can use it as a recovery drive for your Surface device. Having a recovery drive can be crucial if your Surface encounters a situation where it fails to power on, as it might be the only solution to resolve the issue.

**Locate A Misplaced App On The Start Screen.**

Having trouble finding a specific app on your Start screen? Don't worry, you can find it in the "All Apps" section. Simply scroll up from the Start screen until you spot "All Apps." In the list that appears alphabetically, locate your desired app and tap on it to launch it.

If you prefer to have the app readily available on the Start screen for easier access, here's what you can do. Press and hold your finger on the app's icon. Once the app bar appears at the bottom of the screen, select "Pin to Start."

But what if you don't see the option "Pin to Start"? In that case, instead of tapping the "Find on Start" icon on the app bar, touch the "Find on Start" icon on the Start screen. You'll notice that the tile for the previously missing app now has a white border around it, making it more noticeable.

**You Can Add More Storage To Your Surface.**

One of the biggest challenges when transitioning from a desktop PC to a Surface is managing the available storage space. While the Surface Pro 2 offers storage options of up to 512GB, most Surfaces typically range between 32GB and 128GB.

The simplest, fastest, and most effective way to increase storage on your Surface is by inserting a microSDXC memory card into the dedicated memory slot.

However, if you don't have a memory card at hand, here's what you can do to free up space by removing unnecessary files:

1.  Open the Disk Cleanup program from your desktop.

2. In the search field of the Charms bar, type "free up disk space." Then, click on the corresponding link that appears below the search box to launch the disk cleanup software.

3. Click the "Clean Up System Files" button located at the bottom of the window.

4. Select the checkboxes next to the items you wish to remove.

5. Tap the OK button to delete the selected files.

It's important to note that once you delete these files, they are permanently gone. Unlike other files on your desktop, there is no way to recover them.

**Fill Out Your Contact Information On Your Surface.**

To enhance the security of your Microsoft account, it is crucial to select a strong password that prevents unauthorized access to your device through the lock screen. However, what if a kind-hearted individual finds your Surface but doesn't know how to return it to you?

To address this situation effectively, you can employ a quick and straightforward solution by using a permanent marker to write your name and phone number on the back of your Surface. This ensures that anyone who discovers it will immediately notice your contact information and increases the likelihood of its safe return. Additionally, it serves as a deterrent to potential pawn shop dealings.

Alternatively, if you wish to maintain the market value of your Surface, there is another approach you can take. Utilize a graphics editor like Paint on your desktop to add your name and phone number to the lock screen wallpaper you have chosen. This method allows for easy updating if your phone number changes in the future.

By employing this method, whenever your Surface is powered on, anyone who finds it will be able to view your contact information and reach out to you promptly.

# CHAPTER 27:

# HOW TO USE YOUR SURFACE PC AS A PORTABLE DISPLAY: METHOD 2

Do you own a Surface PC? With its mouse, keyboard, touch, and pen support, you have the ability to transform your Surface into a stunning, portable wireless display or a secondary screen.

In this tutorial, I will guide you through the process of connecting and configuring your Surface PC to function as a portable wireless display.

## 1. Set Up Your Surface Pcs

Before proceeding, ensure that both Surface PCs meet the following prerequisites:

- Running Windows 10 with the Anniversary Update or a more recent version.
- Connected to the same wireless network.
- Surface PCs utilizing the Miracast protocol are compatible with this setup. Please note that the first Surface RT model does not support these protocols.

Let's begin the setup process.

## 2. Configuring A Surface PC As A Portable Monitor

Setting up your Surface PC as a wireless display involves the following steps:

1. Open the Settings menu.
2. Select the "System" option.
3. Click on "Projecting to this PC."

4. Choose either "Available everywhere" or "Available everywhere on secure networks" from the first selection.

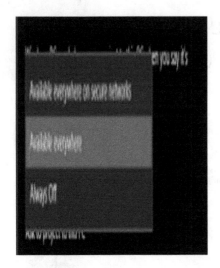

5. From the second selection, opt for either "First time only" or "Every time a connection is requested." If you prefer to avoid constant confirmation for each connection, select "First time only."

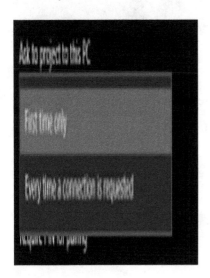

6. For enhanced security, enable the "Required PIN for pairing" feature.

7. If you intend to use your Surface PC as a portable display, ensure that the option "This PC can be found for projection only when it is plugged in" is turned off.

8. When projecting from another computer to this PC, you will be prompted to confirm with a "Yes" response.

## 3. Getting The Surface PC To Show On A Wireless Display

Connecting your Surface PC to a wireless display requires the following steps:

1. Open the Action Center.

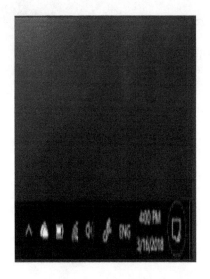

2.  Locate and press the "Connect" button.

3.  Choose the name of the PC you wish to project from, ensuring it is within range. If the connection fails, consider testing the connection on another PC and retrying.

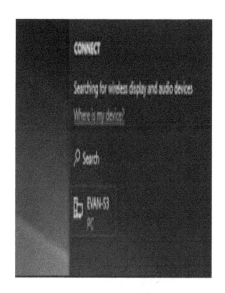

4. Once connected, you have the option to enable "Allow input from a keyboard or mouse connected to this display." This allows you to use the remote computer's mouse, keyboard, touch, and pen input on your main PC.

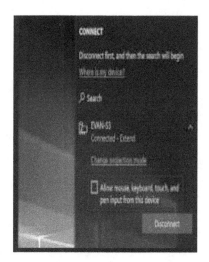

5. You can adjust the projection mode by clicking on "Change projection mode" or using the Win+P shortcut on your keyboard, similar to how you would configure a physical monitor.

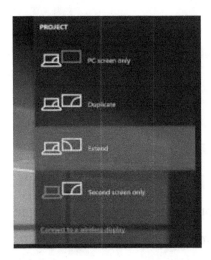

6. To end the connection when you have finished working, simply click on "Disconnect."

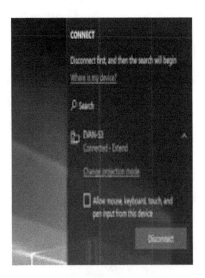

By following these steps, you can successfully project your Surface PC onto a wireless display.

# CHAPTER 28:

# HOW TO ADJUST SCREEN BRIGHTNESS ON SURFACE PRO

The Microsoft Surface Pro is a versatile 2-in-1 device that can function as both a tablet and a laptop. By attaching a compatible Surface Type Cover, it seamlessly transforms into a fully functional laptop. With its laptop-like capabilities and the convenience of a portable tablet, it offers an exceptional user experience. Furthermore, the Surface Pro allows for touch interactions and offers the ability to write directly on the screen.

For those who are new to Microsoft Surface devices or the Windows ecosystem, navigating the device's settings may seem challenging. Adjusting screen brightness, for instance, may not be immediately apparent. In this tutorial, we will guide you through three simple methods to modify the brightness of your Surface Pro screen, whether you have a keyboard attached or not.

## 1. Adjusting Surface Pro Brightness: With Windows Quick Actions

Changing the brightness on your Surface Pro is a straightforward process, especially if you don't have a Type Cover attached. Here's how you can do it using Windows Quick Actions in Windows 10 or Windows 11:

1. Press the Win+A keys together to open the Action Center.

2. Locate the "Quick Action" icon on the right side of the taskbar.

3. Use your finger or the mouse pointer to interact with the slider.

4. Adjust the brightness by moving the slider to the left or right.

5. The slider allows you to set the brightness level on a scale of 0 to 100.

## 2. Adjusting Surface Pro Brightness: With Windows Settings App

Adjusting the brightness of your Surface Pro screen is also possible through the Windows Settings app in Windows 10 and Windows 11. Follow these steps:

1. Begin by launching the Settings app. You can find it in the Start Menu and open it.

2. Within the Settings app, navigate to the "System" section and select "Display" from the list of options.

3. Look for the brightness slider and interact with it using your finger or the mouse pointer.

4. To adjust the brightness, simply move the slider's pointer left or right. This allows you to set the brightness level within a range of 0 to 100.

## Adjusting Surface Pro Brightness: With Surface Pro Type Cover

the Surface Pro Type Cover offers a quick and effortless solution. With a single tap, you can change the brightness by 10 steps. However, it's worth noting that the design of the Surface Pro Type Cover has evolved over time, so you may require assistance in locating the keys responsible for adjusting the brightness.

## 3. Surface Pro 10 Type Cover

The Surface Pro 10 and Surface Pro X Type Cover have been revamped to match their new dimensions, sporting a fresh appearance. On the new Type Cover, you'll find dedicated buttons on the F6 and F7 keys that allow you to adjust the screen brightness conveniently.

To increase the brightness of the screen, simply tap the F7 key. Conversely, to decrease the brightness, tap the F6 key. These intuitive controls provide a straightforward way to modify the screen brightness on your Surface Pro 10 Type Cover.